Victorian Panorama

Ditq - Dnq
Donum Dedid
Nigel.

July 1940.

A Uniform Volume

ROYAL PROGRESS

One Hundred Years of British Monarchy

By

HECTOR BOLITHO

Containing 112 pages of Letterpress and 141 Illustrations, 6 of them in Colour, from old prints and paintings and from photographs, depicting every aspect in the Life of the Monarchy from the Accession of Queen Victoria in 1837 to the Coronation of George VI in 1937. With a coloured jacket by A. T. Barbosa.

Demo 8vo, cloth gilt, 7s. 6d. net.

"An impartial, an accurate, a human, and interesting account of the Royal Family during the last century. The illustrations and photographs throughout are very pleasing. It stands high among the books called forth by the Coronation."—*The Manchester Guardian.*

"*Royal Progress* is quite enchantingly illustrated with 141 plates, which in themselves are worth seven and six."—*The New Statesman and Nation.*

"A beautifully illustrated and intelligently written 'cavalcade' of monarchs from Victoria to George VI."—*The Liverpool Daily Post.*

Published by

B. T. BATSFORD LTD.

15 North Audley Street, London, W.1

1 VICTORIA, THE WIDOW

Photograph by Downey
Decoration by Osbert Lancaster

Victorian Panorama

A Survey of Life & Fashion
from Contemporary Photographs

with a Commentary by
Peter Quennell

LONDON
B. T. BATSFORD LTD.
15 NORTH AUDLEY STREET, W.1

By the Same Author

BAUDELAIRE AND THE SYMBOLISTS
THE PHOENIX KIND
A SUPERFICIAL JOURNEY THROUGH TOKYO AND PEKIN
SYMPATHY, AND OTHER TALES
BYRON: THE YEARS OF FAME, ETC.

First Published, October 1937

MADE AND PRINTED IN GREAT BRITAIN
FOR THE PUBLISHERS, B. T. BATSFORD LTD., LONDON
BY JARROLD & SONS LTD., NORWICH

Foreword

To catch up with reality—somehow to seize the stuff of experience and pin it down—almost since the dawning of personal consciousness has been one of the chief preoccupations of the human race. If only the escalator could be temporarily halted! Hurried in this direction we see moving rapidly, inevitably the opposite way, all kinds of landscapes which are a part of us yet which we are doomed, after a very brief acquaintance, to say good-bye to. The moment is real; yet the moment lasts only sixty seconds; and, rooted to the escalator, smoothly descending towards our goal, we begin to doubt if it had any valid existence. Hence the fascination of modern photography. A shutter clicks; and there, caught and registered by the camera's inquisitive but impartial eye, is at any rate the appearance—the outward *simulacrum*—of such-and-such an occasion, such-and-such personages, such-and-such a now vanished point of view. Processions pass: faces emerge: prospects unfold. The vision of the camera is superficial; but it is to superficialities—to the show, rather than to the inner meaning of things—that the human spirit is most permanently attached. A moment becomes solid on sensitised paper. When Alphonso of Spain —the present Don Alphonso—was driving to his coronation, a loyal subject prepared to take a photograph of the *cortège* as it passed beneath his balcony. It approached, but just as the outriders had drawn level with the balcony, a terrific explosion shook the street and the shutter of the apparatus was released without the amateur photographer being aware that he had made any deliberate movement. The resultant snapshot was an extraordinarily dramatic picture—perhaps the finest news-photograph ever produced. Here we see the faint drifting smoke of the bomb—the wounded coachman reeling upon his box—the foremost horses falling, while members of the cavalry escort which surrounds the carriage rear, prance and subside in the various attitudes of an old-fashioned battle-fresco.

Since that period, the art of the photographer has made prodigious strides, and there are nowadays few aspects of the contemporary scene which have not been illustrated with a wealth and complexity of detail that an historian of the future may not find positively bewildering. But it is not only the historian whom the photographer benefits. Surely, no curious student of human emotions can have failed to respond to the charm—and, now and then, to the pathos —that is to be discovered in a collection of old photographs. For in them we observe the past viewed as the present. The personages who compose these groups—the women who spread their skirts on the steps of country houses, the tourists who stroll down busy streets, the friends or relations who confront the camera linked arm in arm—all inhabit an eternal present; yet that present—like the present enjoyed by the figures on Keats's Grecian urn—is immobile, change-less, ever-enduring. So far has reality been brought to a standstill. Even when we open the family photograph-album we are amazed, and sometimes a little horrified, by an array of selves which, though all unmistakably *our*self, are as dead and forgotten as people of the Stone Age. Just as Dr. Beebe explores the secrets of the submarine universe, so the camera's lens serves as our look-out into a vanished world.

In compiling this volume, we have attempted to compile the family photograph-album of an entire age. It is very far from complete; but, where gaps occur—and gaps are numerous and evident—it is hoped that the reader will supply his own bridge, that he will allow his imagination to wander at will across a past which, although to-day it may seem stuffy, ridiculous and superannuated, was once dis-turbing, exciting and troublesome as the present century. Too often we are inclined to think of the Victorian epoch as having monopolised all the prejudice, self-complacency and fatuous contentment of preceding and succeeding eras. Quite the reverse is true. The Victorian heyday was a period of change; and, though that change was unmarked by any violent political revolution, periods of change are never tranquil, and the lack of tranquillity is reflected in private life. There is a hint of strain about many of these photographed faces, which contrasts oddly with the sobriety and dignity of their customary postures.

Peter Quennell

[vi]

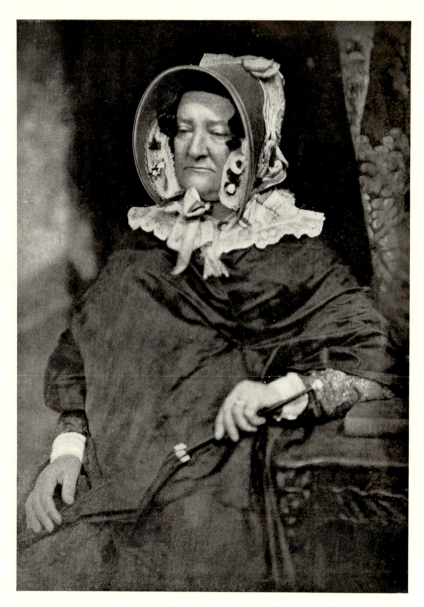

4 Octavius Hill: an Old Lady

2 Street Photography, 1877

3 Studio Photography, 1860

Contents

Acknowledgment

THE Publishers must begin by thanking the authorities of the Science Museum, South Kensington, for the care and courtesy they have shown in producing prints from the fragile early negatives of the Fox-Talbot subjects in their possession, reproduced on figs. 5, 6, 45, 46, 47, 54, 55, 56, 88, 125, 126, 127, 128, and 129. These subjects form a valuable and unique feature of the illustrations, as do the group of portraits which Mr. Guy Little has very kindly allowed us to include from his fine private collection, which are reproduced on figs. 21, 63, 64, 65, 68, 69, 70, 71, 72, 73, 74, 76, 77, 78, 79, 80, 81, 82, 98, 99, 100, 101, 102, 103, 104, 105, 107, 108, 109, 110, 111, 112, 113, 114, 115, 116, 117, 118, 119, 120, 121, 122, 141, 144, and 145. For the Octavius Hill subjects on figs. 4, 7, 8, 12, 13, 48, 50, 51, 52, 53, 61, 62, 89, 90, 130, 131, 132, and 152 we are indebted to Mr. F. C. Inglis, of Edinburgh; for the Crimean War subjects on figs. 85, 86, 87, 93, and 94 to the Proprietors of *Country Life*; for the Indian and Oriental subjects on figs. 83, 84, 91, and 92 to Mr. G. A. Catt; for the group on fig. 44 to Mr. Hector Bolitho; for the subjects on figs. 14, 49, 106, and 138 to the Royal Photographic Society; and for the subject on fig. 151 to the Victoria and Albert Museum.

Among the remainder of the photographs, figs. 1, 42, 58, 75, 147, and 149 were supplied by Messrs. W. & D. Downey; figs. 135, 137, and 143 by Messrs. Thomas Fall; figs. 15, 16, 19, 27, 29, 30, 31, 32, 33, 38, 39, 41, 59, 60, 124, 133, 134, 136, 139, 140, 146, and 148 by the General Photographic Agency; figs. 43, 66, 67, and 150 by Messrs. Gibson, of Penzance; fig. 142 by Mr. H. H. Hole; figs. 9, 10, and 11 by Nadar, of Paris; figs. 153 and 154 by the Rischgitz Agency; figs. 37 and 123 by Sport and General; figs. 18, 28, 34, 35, and 36 by Mr. Will F. Taylor; fig. 57 by *The Times*; and figs. 40, 96, and 97 by Topical. Others are from the Publishers' collection.

1

The Beginnings of Photography

I

TOWARDS noon the more leisured citizens of any Italian community have a habit of retiring indoors. All along the street shutters are closed. The cool, tile-paved, dampish rooms, with their high, dusky ceilings, are given up to silence and shadow; while the sun, making its way through an occasional crevice, describes a thin, burning stroke across the floor.

From this habit, peculiar to the warm countries of the Mediterranean, where light is sharp, shadows so deep that they seem almost solid, and the horizon a jagged knife-edge against the sky, springs an art that was afterwards brought to perfection in the cooler, mistier latitudes of northern Europe. For it was discovered—accidentally no doubt—that, if the room were in complete darkness, a hole pierced through the shutter would project on to the opposite wall an inverted representation of the street outside, and that, by the adjustment of mirrors and lenses, the image could be cast, right way up, on to a horizontal plane—say, a large table—so that it formed a moving and colourful panorama of real life.

Here was the sky, with its birds and clouds; the sunny street, with pedestrians and vehicles. . . . To Giovanni Battista della Porta, a Neapolitan savant who died in 1615, usually goes the credit of the discovery; but a learned French author has pointed out that a detailed description of the camera obscura is to be found among Leonardo da Vinci's scientific manuscripts. It has been suggested even that Roger Bacon, in the thirteenth century, had already glimpsed the possibilities of this simple but extremely fascinating device. But Porta, at least, is responsible for having popularised it. His *Magia Naturalis*, which contained a full account of the discovery, enjoyed an extensive circulation; and henceforward the camera obscura became a fashionable scientific toy.

A toy for many years it was to remain. Speculative rather than analytical, savants of the sixteenth and seventeenth centuries had no definite notion of how the pictures were thrown, and continued to regard the image in the camera obscura as a quasi-magic operation by the sun's rays. They made no attempt to amplify the discoveries of Giovanni Porta; and it was not until the conclusion of the nineteenth century that Thomas Wedgwood, third son of Josiah Wedgwood the potter, assisted by Humphry Davy, endeavoured to fix these "sun-pictures" with the help of chemicals sensitive to the effects of light. Their experiments were enterprising but rudimentary. After coating paper or leather with a weak solution of silver salts, they laid various objects upon the prepared ground. The exposed parts blackened, producing a kind of silhouette in reverse. Wedgwood and Davy next applied themselves to glass-paintings. On one occasion, they placed a sheet of sensitised material in the camera obscura; but the result was disappointing. And Davy and his assistant laboured under the additional disadvantage of not being able to fix the image once it had been obtained. Very soon, the whole sheet would begin to cloud over and their fragile wraith-like images to fade away.

So much for false starts. The real history of modern photography traces its origins to the researches of Niepce and Daguerre in France, and Talbot in England. Both Niepce and Daguerre were customers of the same Parisian optician, from whom they bought their apparatus and supplies. Daguerre was a successful scene-painter who, like many other artists of the period, had employed the camera obscura to enable him to draw landscapes. Hearing that Niepce was at work on similar lines, he wrote to him—Niepce was a prosperous amateur, established at Châlon-sur-Saône—and suggested that they should collaborate. Niepce was suspicious; but Daguerre was persistent. A partnership was at length arranged; and it is to their collaboration, which lasted till Niepce's death in 1833, that we owe the birth of the Victorian daguerrotype.

The fate of the unknown genius—a gaunt, shabby young man—who unpocketed a photographic view of Paris some ten years before Niepce or Daguerre had obtained any satisfactory results, is lost in the obscurity that surrounds the fate of many other ambitious but impoverished inventors. One day, he appeared at the shop also frequented by Niepce and Daguerre and inquired the price of an expensive camera. He could not afford it; and, after hesitating

[3]

in a timid and crestfallen way, he explained that he had been experimenting with the image in the camera obscura and had made good progress but was held up by the deficiencies of the apparatus at his disposal. Then, timidly, he pulled out his soiled pocket-book and showed the tradesman a picture recognisable as neither engraving nor drawing. . . . The optician was impressed. He admitted his interest. The young man restored the picture to his pocket-book and promised to come back; but he did not keep his promise, and the only relic that he left behind was a bottle of some strange blackish solution, which the recipient presently handed to Daguerre, and which Daguerre failed to put to any use.

Presumably, this photograph had been made on sensitised paper. Daguerre himself employed metal; and his first triumph was scored when a silver plate, which had been exposed to iodine vapour and then put away—after an apparently unsuccessful experiment—in a dark cupboard that happened to contain a bath of mercury, revealed on subsequent examination an image far sharper, brighter and more homogeneous than any he had yet achieved. . . . It is not the purpose of this book to give a detailed account of the history of photography or an exact description of early photographic processes. Our concern is with photography in its human aspect; and, having glanced at its beginnings in the work of Niepce and Daguerre, we must turn to the achievements of William Henry Fox Talbot, an Englishman of the type often produced by the liberal yet aristocratic traditions of the late eighteenth century. To these traditions Talbot added the inquisitive scientific temper of the new age. A leisured amateur, he possessed an aptitude for careful

[4]

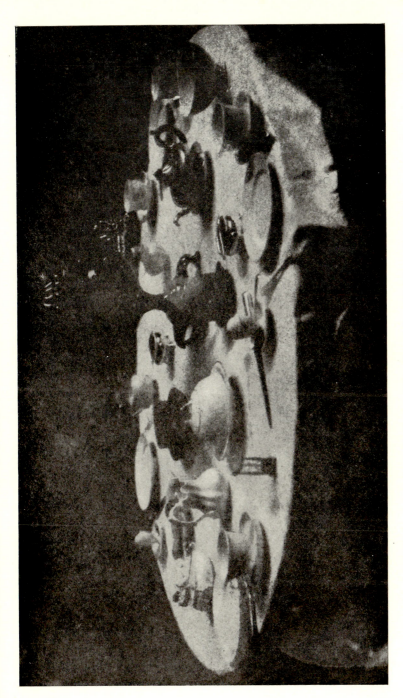

5 Fox-Talbot: The Breakfast Table at Lacock

6　Fox-Talbot:　Mother and Children, 1842

research that led him from dilettantism to scientific discovery. On a tour among the Italian lakes, in pursuit of the picturesque, he had taken with him a small instrument—a development of the camera obscura—known as the camera lucida, which cast a representation of the landscape on to a sheet of paper. But his efforts to pencil over the image proved futile; and when at last, after much diligent scribbling, he removed the sheet, he found that "the faithless pencil had only left traces on the paper melancholy to behold. I came to the conclusion that the instrument required a previous knowledge of drawing, which, unfortunately, I did not possess."

Just as unhappy were his experiences with the camera obscura, to which he next transferred his attention. Struggling to record its imagery with patient but inexpert fingers, he was tormented by the beauty he could not pin down—"the inimitable beauty of the pictures of Nature's painting"—and determined that he must learn to reproduce them by some other and more reliable means. Talbot was not acquainted with the experiments of Wedgwood and Davy and had no inkling of the work that was then being done in France. He knew, however, from his scientific reading, that nitrate of silver was sensitive to the action of light; and his first step was to expose a sheet coated with nitrate of silver; for which he substituted chloride of silver when he discovered that the action of light on the former was much less rapid than he had anticipated. Many experiments were necessary before Talbot produced the type of photographic paper that suited his plans. To begin with, his efforts were unambitious; but, after a time, he decided that he was ready to expose his paper in the camera

2

obscura, and this, after an hour or two, obtained the ghostly representation of a house. "The outline of the roof and chimneys against the sky was marked enough; but the details of the architecture were feeble, and the parts in shade were either left blank or nearly so."

It would be impossible here to chronicle the various experiments through which Talbot fumbled his way to success—the different methods he employed, his hopes, disappointments and speculations; until—in the same year and month as Daguerre, January 1839—with the help of Michael Faraday, who read a paper on the subject before the Royal Institution, he published his discovery to the world at large. Daguerre, meanwhile, had attempted to float a company, had failed and had finally sought the advice of Arago, one of the greatest European scientists of the period, who persuaded the French Government to grant a pension both to Daguerre and—since his partner was dead—to Niepce's son. Daguerre himself took out an English patent and sold licences to practise the new art for as much as a thousand pounds apiece.

Whereas Daguerre reaped celebrity unlimited almost as soon as his invention had been made public, Talbot was obliged to content himself with a more modest *succès d'estime*. His fame was limited to a circle of scientists and scientific amateurs at a time when studios for the exploitation of Daguerre's process were being opened in every large European city. Yet, of the two processes, the calotype (or Talbotype) as Talbot's pictures came to be entitled, was much the more advanced; for while the daguerrotype consisted of a single image, expensive and difficult to make, impossible to reproduce, Talbot had already reached the

[6]

7 Octavius Hill: The Greyfriars Cemetery, Edinburgh
The figure on the left is reputed to be Ruskin

8 Octavius Hill: Miss Rigby

idea of the photographic negative, from which any number of copies might be taken.

For the moment, nevertheless, the daguerrotype gave a clearer and more detailed rendering of real objects. And it was the fidelity and veracity of the new art that fascinated contemporary admirers as they gazed at a portrait where every flower on a shawl, every wrinkle in a satin bodice, emerged brilliant and distinct—or at a street-scene where the cobble-stones glistened after a shower and the painted names could be read above the shop-fronts. Soon caricaturists were ridiculing the enthusiasm with which the great public rushed to have itself portrayed. A satirical lithograph of 1840 shows a vast and frenzied crowd—men and women, young and old, soldiers and civilians—fighting their way into the photographer's studio; while a steamboat is being loaded with photographic apparatus; and a primitive train, drawn by a tall-funnelled locomotive, goes puffing off into the distance, carrying the benefits of photography to foreign lands. The popular response was enthusiastic and immediate. But it must be remembered that, quite apart from the expense, a photographic sitting entailed almost intolerable discomfort. At first, the sitter was often obliged to whiten his face; and it was necessary to remain absolutely motionless, the back of the head clamped in a kind of dentist's vice, till the muscles had grown rigid with suspense and fatigue.

II

After a lapse of more than nine decades, it is scarcely possible to recapture the emotion with which these early photographs—daguerrotypes or calotypes —were passed from hand to hand. In an age already intoxicated with its own scientific prowess, the discovery came as yet another hint of the vast regions that the human intelligence had still to explore, and represented a further conquest in what promised to be a rapid and victorious campaign. Nature itself, looking out of Talbot's and Daguerre's earliest pictures, seems to wear an expression of gratified bewilderment. The bric-à-brac assembled by Daguerre to form his first experimental still-life subjects—drapery, musical instruments, pieces of sculpture—has the prestige of some fabulous and mysterious treasure-trove: Talbot's breakfast-table, as it emerges from its dusky surroundings, has all the freshness of some meal spread for an angelic guest.

Neither Talbot nor Daguerre was a *great* photographer. Talbot, it is true, produced many charming compositions—views of his own house, Lacock Abbey, and of its garden and outbuildings, photographs of soldiers on parade and of officers and sailors on the deck of an old-fashioned man-of-war; but, although he had been attracted to photography in the first instance because he wished to record the beauties of the natural world, his ultimate concern was with the scientific process rather than with its aesthetic effects. Talbot, however, is directly responsible for having inspired the magnificent work of David Octavius Hill. Just as accident had played a large part in the discovery of daguerrotype and calotype, so accident was to launch one of the most distinguished nineteenth-century photographers on his short but brilliant career. But before we discuss the work of Hill, a reference must be made to Nadar, the French artist who—working between 1850 and 1860, whereas Hill did his best work between 1840 and 1850—compiled a series of portraits, literary, musical and theatrical, which, for beauty, interest and variety, has seldom been surpassed. Hill's sitters were relatively obscure. Nadar, whose ambition—*"élever la Photographie à l'hauteur d'un art"*—caused Daumier to portray him in 1862 swinging over the roof-tops of Paris in the gondola of a balloon, took as his subjects such personages as George Sand, Balzac, Baudelaire, Berlioz, Sainte-Beuve, Rossini and Bakunin. Here the advantages of the photographic medium are particularly evident. No matter how gifted he may be, the portrait-painter, since he is of his period, tends to accept his sitters, if not at their own valuation, at least at the valuation of the age in which both he and his subjects happen to live. Personality is often lost behind a thick period-glaze. . . . Thus, the student of some special literary period will often prefer the photographic to the artistic relics of the age that he is investigating; and, while Nadar's photographs have many of the qualities of a fine portrait, his sitters have lost none of their essential strangeness in the process of representation.

What, for example, could be more revelatory than Nadar's portrait of George Sand, who is photographed wearing a large seventeenth-century peruke, in which she bears a remarkable and sinister resemblance to Louis Quatorze? Just as striking, but somewhat less unexpected, is the celebrated portrait of the author of *La Comédie Humaine*—fat-faced, swart, unshaven, one plump but beautifully modelled hand extended across the bosom of an open-necked and, to all appearances, not particularly clean shirt. Very different are the ascetic features of Charles Baudelaire. Nadar made several studies of the poet. All are noteworthy; and the historian of Baudelaire's life will find that he returns to them again and again, observing the grim, thin-lipped mouth—turned down so perversely at the corners—the furtive, troubled eyes, netted with premature wrinkles, and the general air, half monastic and half satanic, that gave Baudelaire his look of the *mauvais prêtre*.

The distinguishing mark of all Nadar's photographs is that they combine a sort of penetrative genius —which enabled him to seize his various sitters at their most characteristic—with the dispassionate skill of the man behind the machine. For a good photograph *must* be mechanical, in as much as a good deal of its fascination depends on the objectivity with which the machine, as distinct from the artist, performs its function. Many modern photographs fall into the category of bad pictures; whereas Nadar, Hill and certain other photographers of the 'forties, 'fifties and 'sixties, though by no means lacking in pictorial sense, did not underestimate the mechanical side of their business. Their work was a collaboration with a mechanical instrument—not an attempt to become artists by mechanical means.

Yet, as Hill's career demonstrates, photography and painting, during the 'forties and 'fifties, were closely akin. Hill had begun life as a painter. He continued to paint when he had given up photography; and it was aesthetic ambition that first induced him to take an interest in the possibilities of the photographic medium. One must admit that he was an exceedingly poor painter. Romantic sunsets, ruined castles, Highland lakes had been manufactured in his studio

[10]

9 Nadar: Portrait of Baudelaire

11 Nadar: Portrait of Georges Sand

10 Nadar: Portrait of Balzac

year after year and exhibited at the Royal Academy with some measure of success. Then, in the year 1843, occurred that famous General Assembly at which Scotland broke away from the Established Church and the Free Church of Scotland was set up in its stead. Fired with religious and patriotic emotion, Hill determined that he would commemorate this majestic event. The commemoration he had in mind was a gigantic group-portrait, containing no less than five hundred likenesses on a canvas that measured some fifty-seven square feet. To collect material for his task, Hill was advised to have recourse to the art of the calotype, which had been popular in Scotland since Dr. John Adamson, Professor of Chemistry at the University of St. Andrews, produced a calotype picture during the year 1840.

By 1843, when Hill first took up photography in a serious spirit, a Calotype Club had already been founded under the patronage of Sir David Brewster, Professor of Physics at the same university as Adamson, and a friend and close associate of Fox Talbot. Besides the encouragement that he received from David Brewster, Hill was also much more indebted to the help of Robert Adamson—John's brother—who acted as his assistant during the period of his greatest photographic triumphs. There is no doubt that, although it had not enabled him to become a good, or even an interesting, painter, Hill's pictorial training was of the utmost value in his new career. Like Nadar, he had a finely developed sense of human character and an extraordinary aptitude for registering its evanescent expressions. Nadar's portraits are very deliberately posed. Hill's, on the other hand, achieve an extraordinary degree of naturalness—an air of ease and freedom which is all the more remarkable if we remember the primness of the typical daguerrotype and the technical difficulties against which Hill himself was obliged to contend.

Just as Nadar seems to have captured the mood of an entire spiritual epoch—the mood of romantic liberalism that culminated in the revolutionary outbursts of 1848 and died away in the prosperous but ignominious years of the Second Empire—so Hill conveys the genius of his time and place. His background was Edinburgh, at a period when its reputation, intellectual and social, was still high; and if there is one trait common to all his sitters it is a look of pride and independence, of austerity tempered with vitality, of activity allied to dignity, expressed both in the positions they have adopted, the modelling of head, mouth and chin, and in the arrangement of light and shade with which the photographer sets off their natural characteristics to the greatest possible advantage.

A single glance at his portraits will make it clear that Hill was a master of portraiture in the great seventeenth- and eighteenth-century tradition, and that he owed much to certain recent Scottish exemplars of that tradition—notably, Raeburn and David Opie. He employed the same dramatic chiaroscuro. Probably no other photographer has achieved so delicate a gradation from high light to deep shadow; and it is noteworthy that, whereas the modern photographer, with his far more sensitive instrument, often produces an effect of light and shade that is striking and dramatic but, from the aesthetic point of view, not in the least memorable, Hill—using only primitive paper negatives—never descended to an obvious or a meretricious contrast. Indeed, the difficulties and imperfections of the new medium gave his portraits an added subtlety and richness of tone.

That Hill should have been able to combine such delicacy with such intensity—such a degree of definition with such mysterious depths of shadow—remains one of the most brilliant, and indeed one of the most puzzling, features of his photographic work. During the five years that he devoted to photography— between 1843 and 1848—we are told that he often produced as many as two or three pictures a day; and from the huge mass of portraits that he left behind it is extremely difficult to make an adequate selection. Remembering how the wonderful series originated, we turn to the great portrait gallery of learned men and dignitaries of the new Scottish Church. Here white neck-cloths, dark coats, faces and attitudes that bespeak the practice of piety and the habits of authority, provide Hill with material for a range of magnificent yet sober compositions. The rugged image of Professor Alexander Monro—where the light is concentrated on the rough-hewn outlines of nose and jaw, and the lower lip projects as if the sitter were about to enunciate some thunderous contradiction— may be paralleled by the smiling benevolence of Dr. Mackenzie, where exactly the same device—that of concentrating the light from above on the subject's head—is used to produce an impression of old age at its gentlest, the lower part of the picture being enlivened by the white marker that has been inserted among the pages of a massive volume.

From Hill's best portraits, accessories of a distracting and irrelevant kind have been almost entirely excluded. Like the old portrait-painters, nevertheless,

3   [13]

he was fond of enclosing within the frame of his composition some symbol to indicate the scope of his subject's interests; and this symbol often takes the form of a book or pen—the book loosely grasped, with a finger still marking the place, the pen just poised, as if its labours had been interrupted for a moment at the photographer's plea. Hill would appear to have made a special study of the human hand. His hands are always memorable and seem to contain almost as much personality as the face itself, whether they are the long and beautiful hands of Mrs. Bertram, emerging from their delicate black lace mittens, or the knotted and masterful fingers of an aged divine. In his pictures of women, Hill allowed himself greater latitude than in his studies of the sterner sex. Again, the background of his portraits is usually simple; but he makes the most of an Indian shawl, the chintz pattern of a dress, the beauty of stripes and tartans, the charm—on his more elderly sitters—of the white widow's cap that surrounds Mrs. Bertram's severe but pleasant features in a stiff, frosty halo.

At the two opposite poles of Hill's photographic achievement are his portrait of an unknown *Old Lady*, where experience, grief, weariness seem to have been written in every line of the sitter's deeply wrinkled face, and his exquisite picture of *Miss Rigby*, afterwards Lady Eastlake, who leans forward, young, unconcerned, graceful, a faint smile hovering about the corners of her large, shapely mouth. In *Girl with Umbrella*, Hill admits for the first time a small bouquet of flowers—carnations and a sprig of jasmine—which harmonises with the pattern of her dress, the brooches, bracelets, ringlets by which it is diversified. *Two Sisters* has all the fascination, but none of the insipidity

[14]

12   Octavius Hill: Dr. Mackenzie

13 Octavius Hill: Master Hope Finlay

of a Victorian genre picture. Here the photographer is attempting one of his most elaborate and imaginative compositions—a dark doorway, the sleek round heads of the two young girls, a black shawl and a raised ringed hand lifted towards the empty birdcage.

Hill's scope, however, was not confined to posed portraits; nor were his sitters limited to the ladies and gentlemen who visited his photographic studio at Rock House, whence he commanded an extensive view over the Old and New Towns. There are also his occasional pictures of children; and, among these, his portraits of the Finlay family—notably, two portraits of Master Hope Finlay, with straw hat and waisted frock coat—stand out as some of the best and most faithful renderings of childhood ever made. In strong sunlight, Hill found that he needed only a very short exposure. Master Finlay, judging by the naturalness of his position, cannot have faced the camera longer than a few seconds; while there are other pictures in which Hill achieved something that was very nearly a snapshot. Many of his liveliest photographs were taken at a Scottish fishing village. With sympathy and humour, but without a touch of the condescension, sentimental or romantic, that was apt to deform the Victorian attitude towards the lower classes, Hill introduces us to a world of tarry sailors, still wearing the hard hats, canvas trousers and short jackets of the Nelsonic navy, and kerchiefed fishwives, whose striped petticoats, shawls and heavy clogs suggest the viragos of the French Revolution.

In the great majority of Hill's compositions the interest is concentrated on the sitter, to the exclusion of his or her surroundings. But there is one series in which the background was his chief object—the photographs taken in the old Greyfriars Cemetery with its Jacobean tombstones, crowded in among the tall, grim buildings of ancient Edinburgh. Against this background, it amused Hill to pose friends and acquaintances in the costume of the Victorian age; and the result has all the charm and oddity of a painting by Magnasco or some other artist of the seventeenth-century Italian school, where peasants, monks, soldiers, gipsies or bandits are portrayed among the mysterious half-demolished symbolism of a forgotten Roman past.

III

Octavius Hill had no direct successors. No other exponent of the calotype came so near to realising Nadar's ambition; and it is not until we reach the eighteen-sixties that a photographer emerges, capable of continuing Hill's work with something of the same originality and grace. Meanwhile, the solid philistinism of the 'forties had begun to give way to the period of aesthetic expansion heralded by the prophets of the Pre-Raphaelite Movement. Mrs. Cameron was imbued with the spirit of the age. She, too, approached photography from a pictorial standpoint; but, whereas Hill was influenced by the portraits of the late eighteenth and early nineteenth centuries, Mrs. Cameron saw her contemporaries through the eyes of Burne-Jones, Rossetti, Millais and Watts.

From Hill's photographs, a whole philosophy of Scottish—and, more generally, of Victorian—middle-class life might be compiled. Just as Gainsborough and Romney present us with the poetic vision of an idealised aristocracy, at a period when projects of Reform were still confined to the bolder members of

[16]

a discontented opposition, so Hill depicts a wealthy and cultivated *bourgeoisie* that had come into its own with the passing of the First Reform Bill in 1832. Gravity, dignity, stability are characteristic of his sitters. After a lapse of two decades, Mrs. Cameron shows us the same intellectual middle class—but a middle class in process of transformation, touched by the first shadows of modern thought.

Charles Darwin was one of Mrs. Cameron's most prominent subjects. Following a practice introduced by Octavius Hill, the portrait is lighted from above. The eyes, under their heavy bristling eyebrows, are lost in deep obscurity; and attention is concentrated on the smooth, magnificent expanse of the old scientist's cranium, which seems to have developed out of all proportion to the rest of the head. Less straightforward is Mrs. Cameron's treatment of the aged physicist and astronomer, Sir John Herschel, whose haggard, wrinkled features are framed in a thin nimbus of straggling white hair and whose eyes glitter direct into the camera's lens.

Among other members of her small but distinguished circle photographed by Mrs. Cameron during the 'sixties and 'seventies were the violinist Joachim, Carlyle—gaunt, bearded, hollow-cheeked—and Longfellow—very much the romantic poet, a large velvet cloak cast expansively over his left shoulder. In his foreword to an admirable selection of the work of David Octavius Hill published not long ago, a German critic, Herr Heinrich Schwarz, has asserted that, although in some pictures Mrs. Cameron carries on Hill's tradition with a fair measure of success, "most of her pictures already betray the inevitable decline of photography." It is true that, turning over Mrs.

Cameron's photographs, we look in vain for the variety, dignity and vitality of Hill's finest portraits. Here is none of the humour, naturalness and charm that irradiates Hill's famous group of the Scottish divine proselytising a congerie of petticoated fish-wives; none of the brilliant observation that produced the superb picture of Lord Robertson or the delightful study of Robert Bryson opening his snuff-box. In Mrs. Cameron's photographs, feminine sensibility has taken the place of Hill's masculine good sense. But then, Mrs. Cameron's sensibility was of a very high order; and, while one must admit that her talent ran now and then to sentimental picture-making, at her best she had a faculty of composition that many painters of the period might have emulated.

If Hill may be said to represent the integrity and vitality of the mid-Victorian period—a period, that with all its limitations, its philistinism, its arrogance and self-complacency, was yet intensely *alive*—Mrs. Cameron's photographs show a slight weakening of the rigid Victorian mood, the gradual incursion of the *fin de siècle*. Over her personages, as over the personages of Rossetti and Burne-Jones, hangs a shade of languor. In 1865 Mrs. Cameron secured a photograph of Ellen Terry, then a very young girl unhappily married to a celebrated Pre-Raphaelite artist; and in accordance with the canons of Pre-Raphaelite beauty she is portrayed in an attitude at once innocent and abandoned, eyes lowered, head leaning for support against the wall, hand fingering the coral chain about her neck. Already a trace of aesthetic sophistication has begun to tinge the snowdrop sentiment of Victorian girlhood!

14 A Study by Mrs. Cameron

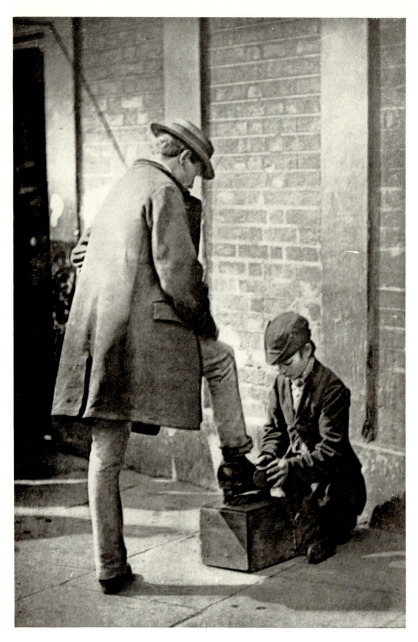

15 The Shoeblack

2

Victorian London

SO prone are we to clothe the idea of Victorianism in the image of what we conceive to be a typically Victorian scene that many of the difficulties—much of the hazard and excitement—of Victorian life pass us completely unnoticed. Thus, London during the reign of Queen Victoria suggests a street of drab, prosperous-looking Victorian houses, each with its area, its portico, its front windows, each façade embrowned by the successive deposits of London November fogs. We think of the sober pavements of South Kensington; but we forget that, while these very houses were being built, "respectable" London was hemmed in by a vast expanse of disreputable outer regions where disease, crime and poverty did their worst.

It would be no exaggeration to say that, between 1810 and 1848, the English ruling classes lived in almost constant fear of some violent revolutionary upheaval. From 1812 to 1816 (when a secret committee reported on the rapid spread of revolutionary feeling among the proletariat and recommended the suspension of the Habeas Corpus Act) the revolution seemed close at hand. In 1832 the riots that preceded the Reform Bill had given rise to equally gloomy apprehensions. In 1848 English Tories had shrunk back alarmed at the speedy and ominous growth of the Chartist Movement; and only exceptional precautions, working in conjunction with the unexampled stolidity of the British temper, saved London from the disorders that broke out simultaneously in Vienna, Paris and Berlin.

Industrialism had created a new universe. Already, in the second decade of the nineteenth century, the introduction of the Frame-Breaking Bill (against which Byron delivered his maiden speech) showed a Tory Government confronted by a situation with which it was not yet competent to deal. The old London mob, which terrorised London during the Gordon riots, had been formidable enough; but the new mob was very different and far more dangerous. It had new and alarming catch-phrases and possessed a bulk, determination and organised ferocity that were the product of years of under-feeding and overcrowding; while behind it loomed the background of the modern slum.

For the modern slum was the natural appendage of the modern industrial city. At an earlier period, when populations were smaller, a certain traditional feeling had penetrated even to the most depressed stratum of the proletariat. Since the Industrial Revolution, every industrial city had opened its gates to an enormous influx of cheap unskilled labour; and this new populace had neither traditions of its own nor respect for the traditions of others. It was needy, and, being needy, became ferocious when, in lean years and by harsh task-masters, it was driven too far. Luckily for the Victorians, it had little coherence; or

16   London Street Arabs of the 'Nineties

17 Ladies of Seven Dials, 1877

the Victorian Age might have developed on unexpected and much less prosaic lines.

Nor is it difficult to understand the fears of well-to-
do church-going Englishmen when we realise the
state of abject misery in which a large section of the
populace were condemned to pass their lives. Let no
one doubt that—both from the humanitarian and
from the utilitarian point of view—the Victorians
were wide awake to the necessity of doing something
to alleviate the condition of the lower classes; but the
problem was so huge that philanthropy, even the
most enlightened, made exceedingly slow progress;
and some idea of the barbarism that still prevailed in
the more congested parts of London as late as the
'fifties and 'sixties may be gathered from this account
of a visit to a typical working-class court off Rosemary
Lane. Access was "through a dark, narrow entrance,
scarcely wider than a doorway, running beneath the
first floor of one of the houses in the adjoining street.
The court itself is about fifty yards long, and not more
than three yards wide, surrounded by lofty wooden
houses, with jutting abutments in many of the upper
stories that almost exclude the light, and give them
the appearance of being about to tumble down upon
the heads of the intruders. . . . At the time of my
visit [writes the investigator], which was in the evening,
after the inmates had returned from their various
employments, some quarrel had arisen among them.
The court was so thronged with the friends of the
contending individuals and spectators of the fight that
I was obliged to stand at the entrance, unable to force
my way through the dense multitude, while labourers
and street-folk with shaggy heads, and women with
dirty caps and fuzzy hair, thronged every window

4

above and peered down anxiously at the affray. There must have been some hundreds of people collected there. . . . On wondering at the number, my informant, when the noise had ceased, explained the matter as follows: 'You see, sir, there's more than thirty houses in this here court, and there's not less than eight rooms in every house; now there's nine or ten people in some of the rooms, I knows, but just say four in every room, and calculate what that there comes to.' I did, and found it, to my surprise, to be nine hundred and sixty. 'Well,' continued my informant, chuckling and rubbing his hands in evident delight at the result, 'you may as well just tack a couple o' hundred on to the tail o' them for makeweight, as we're not werry pertikler about a hundred or two one way or the other in these here places.'"

Such courts were to be found all over London. Soho, Villiers Street leading from the Strand, Berwick Street off Oxford Street, and Golden Square, each had its rookery; Clerkenwell, Whitechapel, Westminster and the Borough were riddled with slum-quarters of the most appalling kind; and the rookery entered from Berwick Street was described as being typical of many others. On one side was a large dust-heap seldom removed—on the other, a water-tank, at which the water was turned on for a quarter of an hour every day; while in a corner stood the latrine that served the whole court.

Many of these slums were extremely ancient; but others—for example, the terrible slums round about King's Cross—had grown up during the last fifty years and covered fields in which Georgian tradesmen had taken the air. By 1891, when Besant published his massive survey of the metropolis, most of the

18 Aldgate Pump in 1880

19 Italian Street Vendors of the 'Seventies

filthier districts had been cleared away; the tangled alleys of Whitechapel no longer enclosed patches of waste land where "the refuse of fish, vegetables, broken baskets, dead cats and dogs" had accumulated in sufficient quantities to "create a fever in any neighbourhood"; and the Fleet River (piped and diverted underground during the 'sixties) had ceased to act as "the common sewer for a population of nearly half a million . . . wafting fever and putrid vapours" from its inky surface.

It was during the 'fifties that London, frightened by the epidemics that tended to break out whenever the weather was warm, first attacked the problem of public health. Thus, in 1849, the *Quarterly Review* had devoted a long article to the condition of London's water-supply and sewers, pointing out that a great part of the present sewer-system dated back to an extremely early period and was either so dilapidated as to be of no assistance at all or quite unfitted to deal with modern needs. Even beneath Belgrave and Eaton Squares, "and the whole splendid neighbourhood of Hyde Park Gardens," were to be found sewers "abounding in the foulest deposits, in many cases stopping up the house-drains and emitting the most disgusting effluvium." St. Giles Rookery, a particularly notorious slum which included ninety-five small houses, split up between two thousand eight hundred and fifty individuals, was often flooded by sewage; while beneath the cloisters of Westminster Abbey lay "a whole network of old cesspools, barrel drains and brick sewers, crammed with five hundred cartloads of stagnant filth."

It is not surprising that outbreaks of cholera and fever should frequently have occurred; and readers of

Bleak House will remember the crusading zeal with which Dickens describes Tom All Alone's, an ancient and pestilential slum in the shadow of Southwark Cathedral:

"Much mighty speech-making there has been, both in and out of parliament, concerning Tom, and much wrathful disputation how Tom shall be got right. Whether he shall be put into the main road by constables, or by beadles, or by bell-ringing, or by force of figures, or by correct principles of taste, or by high church, or by low church, or by no church; whether he shall be set to splitting trusses of polemical straws with the crooked knife of his mind, or whether he shall be put to stone-breaking instead. In the midst of which dust and noise, there is but one thing perfectly clear, to wit, that Tom only may and can, or shall and will, be reclaimed according to somebody's theory but nobody's practice. And in the hopeful meantime, Tom goes to perdition head foremost in his old determined spirit."

And the novelist, working himself up to a pitch of rhetorical exaltation that does not suit his genius very well, proceeds to give an account of Tom's "revenge":

". . . He has his revenge. Even the winds are his messengers, and they serve him in these hours of darkness. There is not a drop of Tom's corrupted blood but propagates infection and contagion somewhere. It shall pollute, this very night, the choice stream (in which a chemist on analysis would find the genuine nobility) of a Norman house, and his Grace shall not be able to say Nay to the infamous alliance. There is not an atom of Tom's slime, not a cubic inch of any pestilential gas in which he lives, not one obscenity of degradation about him . . . but shall work its retribution, through every order of society . . .''

As to the different methods—many of them exceedingly curious—by which the inhabitants of the poorer sections of the richest metropolis in Europe struggled, and often failed, to scrape together some kind of living wage, Mayhew's *London Labour and the London Poor* (published in 1861) contains a mass of extraordinarily interesting information. Lowest of all came a class of men and women who lived on the rubbish and ordures of the city, people who ranged in importance from "Toshers," or sewer-hunters (a comparatively prosperous, though regrettably intemperate, body) to "Mud-larks" and "Pure-finders," both of whom existed close to the starvation-line. It was the pure-finder's business to collect canine excrement from the street and carry it to "the numerous tanyards of Bermondsey, where they sell it by the stable-bucket full, and get from 1s. to 1s. 2d. for it, according to its quality." Between two and three hundred persons were engaged in this nauseous trade, and their average earnings were computed to amount to about seven-and-sixpence a week. Professional mud-larks—the majority being old women and young children—were calculated to number some two hundred and eighty; and it was thought that their individual earnings could not exceed threepence a day. The fall of the tide brought their opportunity; and, as the water went down, they could be seen descending from wharves and stairs all along the Thames, wading through the mud in search of small pieces of coal, chips of wood, "bits of old iron, rope, bones, and copper nails." Iron, bones, rope, nails could be disposed of at adjacent rag-shops; but coals were sold to "the poor people of the neighbourhood at 1d. per pot, holding about 14 lbs." At one of the stairs near the Pool of London, the philanthropic Mayhew assembled about a dozen children apprenticed to the mud-larking business. "It would be almost impossible (he writes) to describe the wretched group, so motley was their appearance, so extraordinary their dress, and so stolid and inexpressive their countenances. Some carried baskets, filled with the produce of their morning's work, and others old tin kettles with iron handles. Some, for want of these articles, had old hats filled with the bones and coals they had picked up; and others, more needy still, had actually taken the caps from their own heads, and filled them with what they had happened to find. The muddy slush was dripping from their clothes and utensils and forming a puddle in which they stood. There did not appear to be among the whole group as many filthy cotton rags to their backs as, when stitched together, would have been sufficient to form the material of one shirt. There were the remnants of one or two jackets among them, but so begrimed and tattered that it would have been difficult to have determined either the original material or make of the garment." Even more miserable was the state of the old women, "especially during the winter, bent nearly double with age and infirmity, paddling and groping among the wet mud. . . . These women always have with them an old basket or an old tin kettle. . . . It usually takes them a whole

[26]

21   The Italian Boy and his Monkey, 1854

20   A Street Doctor, 1877

23   "Public Disinfectors," 1877

22   "Cast-Iron Billy," 1877

tide to fill this receptacle, but when filled, it is as much as the feeble old creatures are able to carry home."

Altogether, a small army of Londoners, men, women and children, scraped a living from the Thames, its muddy and treacherous foreshore, and from the dark underworld of sewers that opened into it. Dredgermen or river-finders, who were often fishermen during the summer months, "either from Barking Creek downwards, or from Chelsea Reach upwards, catching dabs, flounders, eels and other sorts of fish for the London markets," earned a fairly good living by dredging the bed of the river, reaping a harvest of coal, metal, valuables that had fallen into the water from passing craft, and dead bodies—"for which they not only get the reward, but 5s. which they call inquest money." It was a strenuous but un-adventurous life. Sewer-hunting, on the other hand, was attended by very considerable risks; and the experienced tosher must have been a very brave man. In the first place, the toshers' calling was illicit. As late as the middle decades of the century, the mouths of the main sewers, which opened along the riverside, had been entirely unprotected; but, as the river water, particularly during spring tides, had been apt to rush into the sewers and burst up through the gratings into the streets, "flooding all the low-lying districts . . . till the streets of Shadwell and Wapping resembled a Dutch town, intersected by a series of muddy canals," the authorities decided to block the exits, leaving an aperture "covered by a strong iron door, which hangs from the top and is so arranged that when the tide is low the rush of the water and other filth on the inner side forces it back and allows the contents of the sewer to pass into the river, whilst when the tide rises the door is forced so close against the wall by the pressure of the water outside that none can by any possibility enter. . . ."

Through these apertures—which, if they miscalculated the tide, must inevitably close behind them, leaving them to be drowned or stifled—the adventurous band of toshers made their way. "Habited in long greasy velveteen coats, furnished with pockets of vast capacity, and their nether limbs encased in dirty canvas trousers . . . they carry a bag on their back, and their hand a pole seven or eight feet long, on one end of which there is a large iron hoe. The uses of this instrument are various; with it they try the ground wherever it appears unsafe . . . and, when assured of its safety, walk forward steadying their footsteps with the staff. Should they, as often happens . . . sink in some quagmire, they immediately throw out the long pole armed with the hoe, which is always held uppermost for this purpose, and with it seizing hold of any object within their reach, are thereby enabled to draw themselves out." To penetrate the inner labyrinths of the sewer-system, or to venture down any of the ancient and dilapidated side-passages, was considered, even by the boldest and most experienced, an extremely hazardous undertaking. "The brickwork in many places—especially in the old sewers—has become rotten through the continual action of the putrefying matter and moisture. . . . In such parts they are careful not to touch the brickwork overhead, for the slightest tap might bring down an avalanche of old bricks and earth, and severely injure them, if not bury them in the rubbish." Then, of course, there was the danger of foul air. They might lose their way; and, if they were hardy enough to make the expedition

[28]

25   A London Boardman, 1877

24   "Mush-fakers" and Ginger-beer Vendors, 1877

27 Cheapside Flower-girl, 1892

26 Covent Garden Flower-women, 1877

alone, they might be assailed by a horde of ferocious sewer-rats. Men had been terribly bitten; and there was a legend which told how an unlucky tosher had been overwhelmed by his assailants and his bones picked clean.

In return for the dangers that he ran, an experienced and daring tosher could depend on reaping a very profitable harvest all the year round. "There are in many parts of the sewers holes where the brickwork has been worn away, and in these holes clusters of articles are found, which have been washed into them from time to time, and perhaps been collecting there for years; such as pieces of iron, nails, various scraps of metal . . . all rusted together into a mass like a rock, and weighing from a half hundred to two hundredweight altogether." The toshers also brought to light "great quantities of money—of copper money especially; sometimes they dive their arm down to the elbow in the mud and filth and bring up shillings, sixpences, half-crowns, and occasionally half-sovereigns and sovereigns. They always find the coins standing edge uppermost between the bricks in the bottom, where the mortar has been worn away. The sewer-hunters occasionally find plate, such as spoons, ladles, silver-handled knives and forks, mugs and drinking cups, and now and then articles of jewellery; but even while thus 'in luck' as they call it, they do not omit to fill the bags on their backs with the more cumbrous articles they meet with—such as metals of every description, rope and bones." At the end of an arduous day's work, a gang of toshers would retire to the lodgings of whichever member of the party happened to live nearest and count out the spoil. "This done, they then, as they term it, 'whack' the

whole lot; that is, divide it equally among all hands."
Next, they would proceed to enjoy their profits.
"With but ordinary prudence" (Mayhew observes)
it would be possible for them to live well, occupy
comfortable homes and accumulate savings against a
rainy day. "Their practice, however, is directly the
reverse. They no sooner make a 'haul' . . . than
they adjourn to some low public-house in the neighbourhood, and seldom leave till empty pockets
and hungry stomachs drive them forth to procure
the means of a fresh debauch. It is principally on
this account that, despite their large gains, they are
to be found located in the most wretched quarter of
the metropolis."

But the time has come to emerge from the underworld, with its fantastic chivalry of toshers, to the
streets, with their huge floating population of street-
sellers, street-performers and professional mendicants.
Victorian costermongers formed a large and important class. They had their own organisation, their
own standards of conduct, modes of dress, traditions
and prejudices. "The habits of the costermonger
[notes Mayhew, himself a firm upholder of the sancti-
ties of married life] are not domestic. His busy life is
passed in the markets or the streets . . . his leisure is
devoted to the beer-shop, the dancing room, or the
theatre." No less than four hundred public-houses
relied on costermongers for their main source of
revenue; and here they might be seen smoking,
gambling—the last a pursuit of which they were
all passionately fond—playing skittles and shove-
halfpenny, or talking in an odd professional jargon
that made their conversation completely unintelligible
to an outsider. They enjoyed boxing, rat-hunting,

[30]

28   Regent Street in 1880

29 Road Repairs, 1892

30 Newsvendors, 1892

pigeon-shooting and listening to music. They hated policemen and considered that "to serve out a policeman is the bravest act by which a costermonger can distinguish himself." They were staunch radicals and professed an unqualified contempt for the amusements of the aristocracy, but had a pronounced taste for novelettes of high life.

An amiable trait was their devotion to the donkeys who pulled their carts; and many of them resented the ill-treatment of a donkey as they would have resented and avenged an affront to themselves. Indeed, "these animals are not only favourites, but pets, having their share of the costermonger's dinner when bread forms a portion of it, or pudding, or anything suited to the palate of the brute." A certain truculent independence marked them out from other classes of the population; and their dress helped to emphasise their singularity. "A well-to-do coster [writes Mayhew] . . . usually wears a small cloth cap a little on one side. A close-fitting worsted tie-up skull cap is very fashionable just now . . . and ringlets at the temples are looked up to as the height of elegance. Hats they never wear—excepting on Sunday. . . . Coats are seldom indulged in; their waistcoats, which are of a broad-ribbed corduroy, with fustian back and sleeves, being made as long as a groom's, and buttoned up nearly to the throat. If the corduroy be of a light sandy colour, then plain brass, or sporting buttons, with raised fox's or stag's heads upon them—or else black bone buttons with a flower pattern—ornament the front; but if the cord be of a dark rat-skin hue, then mother-of-pearl buttons are preferred. Two large pockets—sometimes four—with huge flaps or lappels, like those in a shooting coat, are commonly worn. If

[31]

the costermonger be driving a good trade . . . he will sport a blue cloth jacket . . . but this is looked upon as an extravagance of the highest order. . . . The fashionable stuff for trousers at the present is a dark-coloured 'cable cord,' and they are made to fit tightly at the knee and swell gradually until they reach the boot, which they nearly cover. Velveteen is now seldom worn, and knee-breeches are quite out of date." In boots and neckerchief the well set-up costermonger took an especial pride; and the whole community— men, women and boys—had a passion for neckerchiefs of brightly coloured silk, a yellow flower pattern on a green ground, or a red and blue design, being particularly popular during the 'sixties. "Even if a coster- monger has two or three silk handkerchiefs by him already, he seldom hesitates to buy another when tempted with a bright showy pattern hanging from a Field Lane door-post."

Besides the costermongers, a vast number of street- sellers added colour and variety to the pavements of the less prosperous London thoroughfares. There were sellers of eatables and drinkables—vendors of fried fish, pickled whelks, hot eels, sheep's trotters, ham sandwiches, pease-soup, hot green peas, penny pies, plum "duff," meat puddings, baked potatoes, spice- cakes, muffins and crumpets, Chelsea buns, sweet- meats, brandy balls, cough drops and cats' and dogs' meat, as well as tea and coffee, ginger-beer, lemonade, hot wine, new milk from the cow, asses' milk, curds and whey "and occasionally water"—hucksters, who dealt in manufactured articles, stationery or second- hand goods, and street-showmen and performers of every kind. The range of the street-showman was extremely elastic. He might exhibit human monstrosities—albinos, dwarfs, giants, spotted boys or pig-faced ladies—extraordinary animals—alligators, pigs and horses with six legs or two heads, industrious fleas or the so-called "happy families," which consisted of a large number of different animals all domesticated to live in the same cage; or he might gratify the curiosity of his public by allowing them to examine "philosophical instruments"—microscope, telescope or thaumascope—new machines for measuring, lifting and weighing, or amuse them with a glimpse of such minor rarities as wax figures, peepshows and glass ships. Street-performers were classified into mountebanks—the Punch and Judy men and the proprietors of fantoccini and Chinese shades—those who dealt in feats of strength and agility—acrobats, equilibrists, tumblers, jugglers, swordswallowers and fire-eaters—the owners of trained animals—dancing dogs, performing monkeys, trained birds and mice, cats and hares, sapient pigs, dancing bears and tame camels—and street-actors and musicians, black-faced clowns and professors of every type of instrument from the dulcimer to the bag-pipes, the old woman who ground away at the hurdy-gurdy and young girls who danced on the stilts in short tartan petticoats.

Every populous street-corner had its crossing-sweeper; and these varied from barefooted boys and girls to venerable top-hatted figures who had established a regular and remunerative pitch in one of the aristocratic squares of the West End, where they extracted a small tribute from passers-by. Many of them found the business not unremunerative. Such-and-such a nobleman had a habit of tipping only in gold: at a certain great house, the butler had been

instructed to see to it that the crossing-sweeper of the
neighbourhood received a substantial Christmas box
every year: and the old man, with his broom and
gnarled forefinger raised deferentially towards the
brim of a battered beaver hat, came to be regarded
as a permanent and respectable part of the splendid
patrician landscape amid which he moved—a fund of
memories and a pillar of tradition.

But a few miles—in some instances, less than a mile
—separated the squalor, confusion and excitement of
the working-class districts from the portentous harmony of Berkeley, Grosvenor, Belgrave and Eaton
Squares. During the sixteenth and seventeenth centuries, rich and poor had been accustomed to live
cheek by jowl, just as to-day, in many Continental
cities, the shop of a small tailor or pastry-cook may be
found wedged into the façade of some haughtily
escutcheoned palace. Englishmen, however, though
they had the reputation of treating their servants
better than other races, had already developed a habit
of keeping their poorer neighbours at arm's length;
and no hint of commerce or glimpse of poverty was
permitted to spoil the aristocratic view. Carriages,
rolling by with wigged coachmen, heavy embroidered
hammer-cloths and large armorial bearings; magnificent flunkeys sunning themselves on whitened door-
steps and exposing to the public admiration their
wonderfully upholstered calves; footmen or foot-boys,
in gold-braided top hats, following their mistress at a
respectful distance, carrying her Prayer Book, lap-dog
or parcel—every detail spoke of wealth and solid well-
being. Hyde Park, as in Captain Gronow's day, was
still reserved for "persons of rank and fashion"; and
during the 'forties this verdant playground of the

[34]

31 Dressed for an Outing, 1895

32 Dressed for an Outing, 1885

33 Happy Hampstead, 1890

rich presented a spectacle that a young Scotsman, visiting London for the first time, found more than sufficient consolation for the sense of loneliness and human insignificance that had overwhelmed him in Piccadilly.

"There is noise there too [writes David Masson, in his pleasant little volume of reminiscences], . . . but, on the whole, all other feelings yield to the exhilaration, the splendid interest and variety of the spectacle. This is London in full season, and in its most glorious conflux; and where in the world besides can there be seen such a gathered tulip-show of radiant faces and dresses, blazing liveries and magnificent equipages? To a provincial, beholding the spectacle for the first time, I am not sure but the horses are as impressive a part of it, as memorable a revelation of the supremacy of the metropolis, as the assembled aristocracy of human beings. Goodish horses are to be seen anywhere; but hardly till one has been in Hyde Park in a late afternoon between April and August, when the stream of carriages is in motion on the carriage-drive, and there are still riders enough in Rotten Row, is the idea of what a horse may be made perfect by abundance of illustration."

To the impressions of a young provincial journalist may be added the London sketches of a foreign poet who had visited the metropolis some ten or fifteen years earlier. We get, first of all, an appreciation of its size, wealth and business; then a glimpse of the appalling abysses of misery and poverty that gaped before the sightseer wherever he went. ". . . Send no poet to London! [complains Heine, in his *English Fragments*.] This downright earnestness of all things, this colossal uniformity, this machine-like movement, this moroseness even in pleasure . . . smothers the imagination and rends the heart. And should you ever send a German poet thither—a dreamer, who stands staring at every single phenomenon, even a ragged beggar-woman, or a shining jeweller's shop— why, then he will find things going badly with him, and he will be hustled about on every side, or even be knocked over with a mild '*God damn!*'"

Coming to the residential parts of the town, he finds their very monotony and the vast extent of ground they cover "wonderfully impressive." Damp and coal-smoke have reduced every brick building to the same "brown olive green: they are all of the same style of building, generally two or three windows wide, three storeys high, and adorned above with small red tiles, which remind one of newly extracted bleeding teeth; so that the broad and accurately squared streets seem to be bordered by endlessly long barracks. This has its reason in the fact that every English family, though it consists of only two persons, must still have a house for itself for its own castle, and rich speculators, to meet the demand, build wholesale entire streets of these dwellings, which they retail singly." Next, he moves on to the West End, where this air of deadening uniformity "is still more dominant . . . where all the houses are as large as palaces, though outwardly anything but distinguished, unless we except the fact that in these, as in all the better class of houses in London, the windows of the first storey are adorned with iron-barred balconies, and also on the ground floor there is a black railing protecting the

[36]

entrance to certain cellar apartments buried in the earth."

Just as the Englishman thrust away his servants into a dark and comfortless basement below the level of the street, so the evidences of poverty (Heine notes) are "crammed away in retired lanes and dark, damp alleys. . . . A stranger who wanders through the great streets of London, and does not chance right into the regular quarters of the people, sees little or nothing of the misery there. Only here and there, at the mouth of some dark alley, stands a ragged woman with a suckling babe at her breast, and begs with her eyes." How different, reflects the poet, in the tone half affectionate, half ironic, that he reserved for every mention of his native land—how different from dear homelike, humdrum Germany! . . . As a pendant to Heine's sketch, it is interesting to turn to the impression of another foreign poet, Paul Verlaine, who visited London during the 'seventies in company with that demonic young man Arthur Rimbaud, just then contemplating the abandonment of his astonishing poetic career. Rimbaud took the first opportunity of buying himself a top hat; but Verlaine, less ambitious, was content to record a genial bewilderment at this city so unlike any city where he had lived, got drunk and written verse before—"*Plat comme une punaise qui serait noire, London! . . . Petites maisons noirousses, ou grands bahuts 'gothiques' et 'vénétiens'* "—and to observe the noisy and ill-mannered street-walkers whom he encountered in flaring public-houses off Oxford Street and the Tottenham Court Road—"*d'exquises miss à la longue jupe de satin groseille, jaspée de boue, tigrée de consommés épandus, trouée de chiures de cigarettes. . . .*"

"*Des cafés propres* [he observes regretfully], *nix,*

6   [37]

nix!" In striking contrast to the life of foreign cities, where pleasures were cheap and public, and where the gaiety of restaurants and cafés overflowed on to the pavements, was the drabness and monotony of Victorian London, in which wealth and privilege kept to themselves and the diversions of the poorer classes were confined to public-houses, music halls, and cider cellars—none of them resorts where the wandering tourist would have found a particularly warm welcome. Prince Pückler-Muskau, whose impressions of English life date from the same period as those of Heine, has left a memorable account of the splendid gloom that prevailed in an exclusive London club. After expatiating on the extreme difficulty of gaining admission, he proceeds to admire the air of subdued luxury that characterised all its appointments—handsome carpets, sheepskin rugs before the doors to shut out the slightest suspicion of a draught, marble chimney-pieces, magnificent looking-glasses—and to describe the embarrassment that he experienced when he learnt that it was the custom to enter "the brilliantly lighted saloon of the club-house, where dukes, ambassadors and lords, elegantly dressed, are sitting at the card-tables," without removing one's hat! Such aristocratic *désinvolture* was hard to absorb. He appreciated nevertheless the extreme ingenuity that well-to-do Englishmen displayed in all questions affecting their own comfort—for example, in the design of club arm-chairs, which were "adapted to every degree of fatigue, indisposition, or constitutional peculiarity. . . . It is a positive pleasure even to see an Englishman sit, or rather lie, in one of these couch-like chairs by the fire-side. A contrivance like a reading-desk attached to the arm, and furnished with a candlestick,

34   Charing Cross and Northumberland House in the 'Seventies

35 Leicester Square in 1883, just before the building of the old Empire

is so placed before him, that with the slightest touch
he can bring it nearer or further, push it to the right
or to the left. . . . A curious machine, several of
which stand around the large fire-place, receives
one or both of his feet; and the hat on his head
completes this enchanting picture of superlative
comfort."

So much for strongholds of St. James's Street and
Pall Mall. Prince Pückler-Muskau—like Verlaine—
had a very poor opinion of the English theatres, which
struck him as smelly, stuffy and overcrowded; and the
nineteenth-century Londoner who looked for some
type of amusement more Bohemian than that provided
by the legitimate stage—where, during the 'forties,
Taglioni might be seen dancing in classical ballet or
Jenny Lind, "a wild, fair-haired fawn of genius, all
gold and goodness, from her native snow-clad hills,
looking round with scared eyes, stepping rhythmically
and beating her little drum"—probably gravitated to
a squalid and smoky cider cellar. These cellars were
the gathering-place of writers and journalists; and
during the middle of the century it became the fashion
to visit the cellars in Maiden Lane, there to hear "the
great Ross" sing the lugubrious ballad of *Sam Hall*,
which, in different forms, has since spread through
every English-speaking country. It was the singer's
practice to dress and act the part. Looming through
the smoke of pipes and cigars, "a strange, gruesome
figure, in ragged clothes, with a battered old hat on
his head," he would remove his short blackened clay
and, "looking round with a dull, brutal scowl or
glare," begin, "as if half in soliloquy, half in address
to an imaginary audience, his slow chaunt of the
condemned felon":

[39]

And the parson he will come,
   He will come,
And the parson he will come,
   He will come:
And the parson he will come,
And he'll look so blasted glum;
And he'll talk of Kingdom Come:
   Damn his eyes!

—An odd commentary on the tastes of an age more often associated with the singing of sentimental drawing-room ballads.

But the cider cellars were a relic of an earlier time; and, while many reminders of Georgian, Carolean and even Elizabethan London survived till a comparatively late period—for instance, the ancient Cock Inn next to Temple Bar, famous for its admirable port—the centre of the metropolis changed as rapidly as its outskirts spread. Temple Bar itself (against which *Punch* had long conducted a philistine agitation) was removed in 1878; and, although the uprooting of Wren's noble arch might be defended on utilitarian grounds, it is a thousand pities that the intrusion of a hideous railway viaduct should have been allowed to break the once splendid and sweeping view towards St. Paul's up the slope of Ludgate Hill—a prospect particularly beautiful on summer evenings when the last light of the day still clothed the great blue dome of the cathedral and the old house-fronts beneath it were already in shadow.

Meanwhile, the voracious suburbs flung out their tentacles. For many decades they had been growing; and a caricature, executed between 1810 and 1820, makes it quite plain that jerry-building and ribbon-development even then were going rapidly forward.

36 The Café Royal, 1901

37 Shopping in Regent Street, *ca.* 1900

38 Shopping in Westbourne Grove, 1900

39 High Holborn, *ca.* 1900

Here we see a legion of bricks and builders' tools rushing out into the country and putting to flight hedges, haystacks, trees, which retreat in helpless disorder towards the heights of Hampstead. That perverse individualism which ordains that every English family shall inhabit its own tiny brick box and cultivate its own scrubby patch of garden was creating a new ramshackle universe of crescents, squares and groves; and when Don Juan enters London—Byron had left England in 1816—he is impressed not only by its scenes of metropolitan grandeur but by its squalid outskirts which provide glimpses of pretentious suburban desolation:

> Through Groves, so call'd as being void of trees,
> (Like *lucus* from *no* light); through prospects named
> Mount Pleasant, as containing nought to please,
> Nor much to climb; through little boxes framed
> Of bricks to let the dust in at your ease,
> With 'To be Let,' upon their doors proclaim'd;
> Through "Rows" most modestly called "Paradise,"
> Which Eve might quit without much sacrifice.

Besides the photographs of mid-Victorian London, the present survey includes a number of views of London taken during the 'eighties and 'nineties. London was then a shabbier, noisier, grimmer, but perhaps it was also a more individual and interesting city than the impersonal, half-Americanised metropolis that reaches a climax of tedium in Piccadilly Circus and Regent Street as they have been remodelled during the last fifteen years. It was darker, too. The dense yellow fog that plays so important a part in the romances of Jules Verne and Conan Doyle had not yet lifted. Many streets were still paved with granite blocks; the hubbub that impressed George

[41]

Borrow and De Quincey was still prodigious; and the drumming of a thousand wheels and a thousand hooves still reverberated in its narrow, congested arteries—a sound that De Quincey, haunted by recollections of his own unhappy adolescence, could never forget, till he came to identify himself with the suicide buried, a stake through his heart, under the pavement of a busy East End cross-roads—"And over him drives for ever the uproar of unresting London."

40 Off for the Holidays, *ca.* 1900

41 Hotel Chambermaids, 1892

42 Victoria, the Wife and Mother: a Group of the Late 'Fifties

3

Victorian Family Life

FAMILY portraits form one of the most interesting, but also one of the least attractive, departments of Victorian domestic photography. Here are the conversation-pieces of the Machine Age. A certain rigidity may be accounted for by the limitations of the photographer's apparatus; yet the contrast between these conversation-pieces and their Georgian prototypes is not without its own special significance. In most eighteenth-century portrait-groups, however stilted and artificial, we feel that the painter has attempted to convey an air of ease, naturalness and grace. Perhaps a child is playing on the floor; a young girl bends over a scroll of open music; the black servant brings in a pot of coffee; while the lap-dog runs barking at his heels. There is a suggestion of dignity combined with *bonhomie*. . . . Fifty years later, the descendants of these careless, cheerful-looking men and women were facing the cold impersonal eye of the camera in a very different frame of mind. The family seems to have drawn in upon itself. Examining an eighteenth-century portrait group, we are often unable to distinguish at a first glance between the

[43]

various members of the clan. A father would appear to be conversing with his elder sons on terms of complete equality. His attitude may be Olympian; but the deity he represents is Jove in a good humour, his thunderbolts laid aside, the younger gods grouped pleasantly around him. The Victorian paterfamilias, on the other hand, is Jehovah; and, like Jehovah, Victorian Papa, during his public appearances, was sometimes in an exceedingly nasty mood. A danger signal glimmers from beneath his eyebrows: "*I am that I am . . .*" Both hands are laid heavily on massive thighs encased in tight check trousers; a watch-chain, solid, tasteless, but obviously valuable, shines on the majestic bulge of his stomach. Mamma is at his side, the youngest child, its round, innocent forehead ornamented with beer-barrel curls, perched on her knee, and to right and left, and behind his throne, stand his sons and daughters. The girls are subdued and vague and sweet, the boys as impersonal as young saplings round the parent oak. . . .

Just as it is instructive to bracket together the portrait of the bewigged or helmeted founder of a great family with a photograph of the young motor salesman or share-pusher who at present bears the name, so it is instructive to reflect that behind every modern *ménage* loom portrait groups—many portrait groups —of the kind that will be found illustrated in this volume. For such a family was the unit on which the whole fabric of Victorian society was built up. The Victorians, as I have elswhere tried to suggest, were Romantics at heart; and, however prosaic the result, their pursuit of duty and cultivation of the more arduous domestic virtues was carried on with peculiarly romantic thoroughness. Duty, after all, is

43 Middle Class, *ca.* 1870

44   A Croquet Party of the 'Sixties

a romantic ideal. And in opposition to the comparatively cynical and matter-of-fact style in which the eighteenth century attempted to regulate its domestic affairs, the Victorians raised the standard of romantic endeavour. The path of domestic duty was often hard. That a course of conduct was unpleasant suggested to the Rationalists of the eighteenth century that it was unnatural—hence wrong; whereas the Victorians, trained to consider suffering as one of the natural concomitants of an upright and God-fearing life, accepted pain as almost a guarantee of divine approval. Their portrait-groups suggest fortitude rather than gaiety. They are proud to escape the implications of seeming to enjoy themselves.

Thus, there is more character than charm in their photographed faces. Every century the human race appears to change its mask; and the Victorian physiognomy must be included among the most peculiar and distinctive that it has yet assumed. Pinched or broad, spherical or long, double-chinned or lantern-jawed, it is strongly marked and firmly modelled, with deep lines running from the nose and a mouth often dragged down at the corners. The expression may be benign, dignified or merely pompous; but it has a kind of self-assurance in which modern faces are strangely and—at times—sadly lacking. This is a man or woman who knows his or her place, and believes in the rightness of the scheme of society by which that position was ordained. Farmer, merchant or nobleman—each confronts the camera solid and four-square, very much himself and, to judge by his appearance, very comfortably established in the station of life to which it has pleased God to call him. In modern photographs, the attitude of the sitter often hints at a restless dissatisfaction with his or her immediate surroundings. The photographed beauty yearns out of her frame as if she were preparing to fly away to heaven on a cloud of tulle. Shall she sell her title to a firm of cold-cream manufacturers, join a film-company or begin to write a novel? The accessories among which the photographer has seated her are vague and various, and imply the vagueness and variety of the subject's interests. How different from the solid circular table, the open book, the broken classical pillar or cascade of weeping fern!

Among the photographs included in this collection will be found many different aspects of Victorian family life. Here are pictures that show it at its least formal—pleasant groups taken in gardens and on the steps of English country houses—ladies with wide summery crinolines and whiskered gentlemen wearing bowlers or rat-catcher caps. Here, too, are glimpses of our grandfathers and grandmothers at their most unprepossessing. Samuel Butler has described the misery that a thoroughly ill-natured and unimaginative paterfamilias could spread around him; and, lest his account of his own family should be thought exaggerated, the photographs of Mr. and Mrs. Butler should be reproduced in future editions of *The Way of All Flesh*. After studying those grim and snuffy features, no critic can suspect that Butler's portrait of the Reverend Ernest Pontifex was malicious and overdone, or that the tyranny that made such an impression on Butler's later development was not perfectly genuine. Yet even an Ernest Pontifex may have his uses. It is true that with the decay of family life we have escaped much suffering; but it is also true that we have lost a valuable opposition—the rampart of

45 The Tea-table, Early 'Forties

46 A Family Group, Early 'Forties   *Fox-Talbot*

47　On the Lawn at Lacock in the Early 'Forties

Fox-Talbot

Octavius Hill

48 A Household of the Early 'Forties

49　A Grandmother of the 'Forties

50 Children of the 'Forties   *Octavius Hill*

51 Lessons in the Open Air, *ca.* 1845

Octavius Hill

52   Sleeping Child, Early 'Forties

Octavius Hill

53   A Carriage Party of the 'Forties

Octavius Hill

paternal disapproval from which Victorian youth—
Butler among others—bounced off into brilliant
literary flights. Few artists are the worse for something to react against; and, in late Victorian and early
Edwardian literature, we have the spectacle of rebellious young men protesting against Victorianism
with an earnestness and energy that was itself
thoroughly characteristic of the age. For every institution nurtures within itself the seeds of future revolt;
and the more robust the institution, the livelier and
stronger their growth is likely to be.

.   .   .   .   .

The Victorian ideal of marriage is a case in point.
Marriage, says the Prayer Book, is an "admirable
mystery." And, if later periods have been inclined to
study marriage in its mysterious aspect, the Victorians
preferred to concentrate upon its less problematic and
more sacramental character. No need to resusci-
tate Tennyson's verses celebrating the beauties of
monogamous married love. Tennyson's own conduct—though towards the end of his life his talent is
said to have run to the composition of exceedingly
improper limericks—was irreproachable throughout
his long married career; and it was Tennyson who
handed Prince Albert the white flower that marked
him for all time as the type of perfect father and
husband, cleaving to one woman, bringing up a
large and dutiful family, expiring at length amid
the loud lamentations of his nearest and dearest
assembled in various attitudes of distraction around
his bed.

To Coventry Patmore, however, one of Tennyson's
early friends, during the period that followed *In*

Memoriam and preceded the writing of *Maud*, belongs the distinction of having made himself the laureate of Victorian married love. Other poets have spoken respectfully of Hymen; Patmore alone professed to regard uxoriousness as next to godliness, and elevated his worship of marriage to the status of a semireligious cult. The *Angel in the House* is the gospel of nineteenth-century wedlock. It introduces us to the hesitations and aspirations of courtship, the bliss of the engagement when the lovers walking under the chestnut-trees hear the tinkle of a piano on which Mendelssohn's *Wedding March* is being rehearsed:

> Geranium, lychnis, rose array'd
>   The windows, all wide open thrown;
> And some one in the study play'd
>   The Wedding-march of Mendelssohn . . .

the joys of a placid married life, once the angel—now safely domesticated—has folded her wings in the shelter of a quiet and contented home.

Patmore married three times; and, on each occasion, he entered upon the sacred contract in an exceedingly serious spirit. That man and wife should be in perfect harmony with regard to religious and intellectual questions was then considered a matter of the utmost importance; and we learn that Patmore gave his first betrothed a copy of Emerson's *Essays*, and was relieved and delighted to discover that her pencilled annotations precisely corresponded with his own ideas. Thus had Mr. Gladstone and Dr. Arnold proposed to the young women on whom their choice had fallen some problem affecting the grave religious issues of the day. Mrs. Gladstone and Mrs. Arnold, like Mrs. Patmore, had been able to convince

[48]

54, 55 The Servants at Lacock, *ca.* 1842   *Fox-Talbot*

56 The Servants at Lacock, *ca.* 1842

Fox-Talbot

their suitors that their orthodoxy was above reproach; and the calm and fruitful marriages that resulted drew an added sweetness from the thought that the partners shared the same convictions, just as on Sundays they shared the same family pew, and that they were doubly armed against the insidious attacks of Doubt!

But not all the Victorian couples were quite so fortunate; and to turn from the married life of Coventry Patmore to the married life of the great Victorian sage, who, at the time when Patmore first met him, was already an embittered old man, is to exchange the somewhat stifling atmosphere of a connubial paradise-on-earth for the gloom and sulphur-smoke of an almost modern purgatory. Well might Jane Carlyle write of the "Valley of the Shadow of Marriage." But then Mrs. Carlyle was scarcely characteristic of her period, having none of the submissiveness that the Victorian age expected of its women and—to make the situation worse—a sharpness of tongue and an acuteness of insight, trained to demolish sentimentality and pretension in a single sweeping phrase. Her account of the origins of her marriage might have been composed by a modern novelist :

". . . Just because, in virtue of his being *the least unlikeable* man in the place, I let him dance attendance on my young person . . . I came to *need* him—all the same as my slippers to go to a ball in, or my bonnet to go out to walk. When I finally agreed to marry him, I cried excessively and felt excessively shocked—but if I had then said *no* he would have left me—and how could I dispense

8

with what was equivalent to my slippers or bonnet? Oh, if I might write my own biography from beginning to end—without reservation or false colouring—it would be an invaluable document for my countrywomen in more than one particular, but *'decency forbids'*."

One fancies that, in happier circumstances, Carlyle, though he had none of Coventry Patmore's rather superficial romanticism, would himself, perhaps, have developed into a patriarch of the conventional Victorian type; but, married to Jane Welsh Carlyle, he was never able to consolidate the character and remained the somewhat cantankerous prophet of Chelsea—a prophet with little honour in his own home, or with considerably less honour than so dogmatic and authoritative a personage might have claimed as his due.

Dickens was another exception to the Victorian rule. Whereas the Dora celebrated in *David Copperfield* dies in early youth and leaves behind her a pathetic and charming memory, the young woman from whom the novelist took his portrait of the hero's first wife, and whom he himself married, lingered on into a forlorn and rather neglected middle age, still helpless but no longer fresh and attractive. Dickens's interest in younger and prettier women was a subject of some scandal, and it was perhaps an element of duplicity in his private life that gave a certain smug disingenuousness to his treatment of marriage. Thus, *David Copperfield* contains a picture of the perfect Victorian wife studied from two opposite but complementary aspects. Dora is the child wife who arouses her husband's protective and quasi-paternal

57 A Household of the 'Sixties

58 A Party at Balmoral in the 'Fifties

59   Mother and Daughters of the Late 'Sixties

60   At the Seaside in the Early 'Eighties

feelings. "I was such a silly little creature," she admits on her death-bed; and, all through the second volume of the book, up to the harrowing farewell scenes, she continues to display a touching incapacity, which exasperates her husband yet warms his heart. Agnes is Dora's exact antithesis. She is the counsellor, the friend, the devoted and self-effacing helpmate, firm yet gentle, wise yet indulgent, brave yet feminine, the personification of noble Victorian womanhood. She has all the virtues—every moral and spiritual quality. She does everything, except engage the reader's interest.

A last glimpse into the Victorian Garden of Eden. On January 25th 1858 Princess Victoria of England (the Prince Consort's favourite child, whose departure for Germany did much to add to the darkness of his closing years) was married to the Crown Prince Wilhelm of Prussia; and a photograph taken after the ceremony in the gardens of Buckingham Palace gives a pretty picture of a Victorian bride and bridegroom. How gracefully Victoria clings to Wilhelm's sleeve! How knightly is the young bridegroom's expression as he turns to face the camera! With what determination do they seem to be confronting the perils of adult married life! Who could guess that we had before us the future parents of one of the most execrated monarchs in modern European history—that to this marriage we owe the birth of the Emperor Wilhelm III and the ultimate downfall of Victorian moral standards?

61   Sailors, *ca.* 1842   *Fox-Talbot*

62   Scottish Fishwives, *ca.* 1845   *Octavius Hill*

63 Cora Pearl

64 Lord and Lady Hastings

65 Demureness in the *Demi-monde*:
"Skittles"

CHAPTER

4

𝕻ictorian 𝕷ow 𝕷ife

ROM the symphonic background of the mid-
Victorian age emerge certain discordant sounds—
roars of high, tipsy laughter, shrieks of terrified women,
noise of chairs overturned and petticoats rent. Lord
Hastings and an accomplice, having first turned out
the gas-lamps, have suddenly emptied a sackful of
ferocious sewer-rats among the dancers at Mott's
"Night-House" in Foley Street, then made their
escape under cover of darkness, hailed a cab and
driven off to finish an enjoyable evening in the
sympathetic atmosphere of Cremorne Gardens. Such
practical jokes, it is true, even in the fastest, rowdiest
and most fashionable circles, were not very often
played; but the student of Victorianism who imagines
Victorian life to have consisted of one long, flat,
undifferentiated expanse of respectability should
consult some of the sporting chroniclers of the
period or examine the huge quantities of satirical
or semi-pornographic literature that it produced.
During the 'sixties, the whole neighbourhood of
Piccadilly, and the streets that stretched from Piccadilly
southwards, teemed with resorts that combined

the character of modern night-club and eighteenth-century bagnio and gambling hell. The Haymarket "literally blazed with light" till dawn; and the wanderer had his choice between all kinds of eating, drinking, and meeting houses, the Blue Posts, Barnes's, the Burmese and Barron's Oyster Rooms, the latter a particularly famous rendezvous devoted to the guzzling of oysters and the consumption of enormous quantities of dry champagne.

Panton Street was "another very sink of iniquity." It had hot baths of extremely doubtful reputation, and the night-houses which went by the names of Rose Burton and Jack Percival—the latter being, perhaps, a little more respectable than the former, a centre of sporting life where celebrated boxers received friends and admirers after a victory or a defeat. In Arundel Place, leading off Coventry Street, a gang of sharpers, "who made human nature their study, and scoured the highways and byeways nightly in search of profitable quarry," had established their headquarters; and to the quiet, shabby coffee-house that they frequented they were in the habit of bringing back rich, guileless young men who wished to try their luck at the three-card trick or *chemin de fer*.

Kate Hamilton's was universally notorious. The visitor approached by a long tunnel-like passage, guarded by two janitors, pressed a bell, and was admitted—after scrutiny—into a large gas-lit saloon, dominated at one end by the mistress of the house, who sat upon a small dais, sipping champagne and issuing her orders in a "fog-horn voice." Kate Hamilton was the typical *meretrix* of legend. Old, ugly, bloated—with "as hideous a physiognomy as

[54]

any weather-beaten Deal pilot"—she affected very low-cut evening dresses and "shook like a blancmange every time she laughed." "Bobby, my dear, come and sit by me," she would intone, half wheedling, half commanding; and the young officer or landowner on whom her attention had fallen would take the favoured place beside her throne; while champagne would be drunk at his expense by the entire company.

Mott's made as large a haul of youthful innocence. It was the preserve of the dissipated aristocracy, who obtained an entrance "as it were by right," while "parvenus, however wealthy," were refused the door. Only successful actresses and the most expensive and accomplished courtesans were permitted to join this splendid gathering; and, among the women who decorated the dance-floor and the supper room, "Skittles," celebrated for the beauty of the ponies that she drove in Hyde Park and St. John's Wood, and "Sweet Nelly Fowler" were the principal stars. "Skittles" was a practical and forthright person; but the stories that attached themselves to "Sweet Nelly Fowler" were much more elegiac; and it was believed that she "had a natural perfume, so delicate, so universally admitted" that young men who were in love with her "paid large sums for the privilege of having their handkerchiefs placed under the goddess's pillow, and sweet Nelly pervaded—in the spirit, if not in the flesh—half the clubs and drawing-rooms of London."

At the Cremorne Gardens the prospect of finding agreeable company was sharpened by the likelihood of becoming involved—sooner or later—in an exhilarating free fight. On a Derby night (says the historian

9*

of the 'sixties) the gardens "baffled description"; the *Hermit's Cave* and the *Fairy Bower* were "filled to repletion"; while, if one should pass too near to the private boxes, a quartern loaf or a dish of cutlets might very well be hurled at venture at one's head. All the time the atmosphere grew more intense; "a Derby night without a row was, in those days, an impossibility"; and no sensible man thought of entering the Gardens with a watch and chain, or in a coat that he would object to having torn from his shoulders . . . The outburst of the row would occur suddenly— sticks crashing down upon top hats, tumblers flying through the air, "fists coming in contact with anything or anybody whose proximity seemed to suggest it." Then a general exodus—"helterskelter, old and young, Jew and Gentile, soiled doves and hereditary legislators dashed like the proverbial herd of swine towards the gates. Often did this stampede continue for a mile, till straggling cabs, on their way to their stables, picked up the stragglers, and landed them in less disturbed districts. But the night was by no means over . . . for roysterers like Lord Hastings."

After these nights out, Lord Hastings—who plays a heroic and prodigious part in that fascinating book, *London in the 'Sixties*—was usually to be discovered breakfasting off a dish specially prepared for such occasions and known as "Fixed Bayonets." But, at that happy period, opportunities of dissipation—at any rate for the rich and strong-stomached—were considerably more numerous than they are to-day; and a riotous evening at the Cremorne Gardens might be followed by a visit to the races and to the cockpit, or by a hazardous expedition along the Ratcliff Highway. Cock-fighting was still popular in the 'fifties and 'sixties. Though illegal, it was practised surreptitiously in several districts of London; and the author of *London in the 'Sixties* describes how he, Lord Hastings and another celebrated *viveur*, the Duke of Hamilton, accompanied by a bevy of foreign diplomats, joined forces at a subterranean cockpit in Endell Street. There Lord Hastings' bird, "the brave old champion Sweep," won his last battle but "received his quietus"; and, having exhausted this amusement, the party set off on what we are told was "one of the most popular amusements of the long-ago 'sixties . . . going the rounds of the dens of infamy in the East End and the rookeries that then abutted upon the Gray's Inn Road." The Ratcliff Highway was especially attractive. Nowadays a dim and shoddy thoroughfare running through a gloomy but uninteresting quarter, it was at that date a "place where crime stalked unmolested," so much so that "to thread its deadly length was a foolhardy act that might quail the stoutest heart."

Occupied from end to end by drunken sailors, furiously spending the money they had earned on their last voyage, it rang with songs, oaths, quarrels; and all along its length "were dens of infamy beyond the power of description—sing-song caves and dancing booths, wine bars and opium dens, where all day and all night Chinamen might be seen in every degree of insensibility from its noxious fumes." The visitors were accompanied by a detective. "All right, lads, only some gents to stand you a drink," he announced at the door; and in filed the top-hatted, opera-cloaked tourists from the West End, to mix with blousy prostitutes—"drunken women with bloated faces, caressing their unsavoury admirers"—and fierce seamen "of every nationality in long sea-boots, and deadly knives at every girdle."

Even more brutal was the excitement of an execution. Byron and a party of friends had occupied a window opposite Newgate to watch John Bellingham, the assassin of Spencer Perceval, "launched into eternity"; and, fifty years later, an aristocratic party of much the same composition gathered to see the public hanging of the "seven Flowery Land pirates." Rain was falling in torrents when they approached the jail. As far as the eye could reach, "the lowest scum of London"—some two hundred thousand of the most desperate and degraded characters of the entire metropolis—were packed together beneath the walls of the ancient prison, picking pockets and committing highway robbery as it suited their mood. Across the entire front of Newgate a heavy barricade had been erected, built of solid timbers; but this barricade served a somewhat unexpected purpose; since it prevented the police, who for the most part were assembled in the immediate neighbourhood of the scaffold, from coming to the assistance of harmless citizens who found themselves at the mercy of the crowd. "The scene that met one's view [writes a curious spectator] on pulling up the windows and looking out on to the black night and its still blacker accompaniments" was terrifying and indescribable. "A surging mass, with here and there a flickering torch, rolled and roared before one; above this weird scene arose the voices of men and women shouting, singing, blaspheming, and as the night advanced and the liquid gained firmer mastery, it seemed as if hell had delivered up its victims. To approach the window was a matter of danger; volleys of mud immediately saluted one, accompanied by more blaspheming and shouts of defiance. It was difficult to believe one was in the centre of a civilised capital that vaunted its religion and yet meted out justice in such a form."

Not till four o'clock did the ministers of justice begin to appear. There was a rumbling of cart wheels— the dull thud of hammers and carpenters' mallets; and, through the rainy murk that hung over the heads of the mob, a gang of labourers, working by lantern-light, were seen putting the finishing touches to the structure of the scaffold. Then, unobtrusively, the "Debtors' Door" was opened; and, from this exit, which led to the scaffold through the prison kitchens, peeped out an ancient and decrepit man, who sidled forth, cautiously tested the drop and (followed by roars of execration) quickly slipped back into the prison whence he had come. At half-past seven, St. Sepulchre's bell started its tolling. The solemn strokes of the bell, added to the ominous knocking of the workmen and the distant hubbub of a savage and excited crowd, must have combined to give a peculiarly tragic intensity to the atmosphere that prevailed within the prison. A few last preparations—sand scattered near the drop, lest the minister of religion attending the prisoners should lose his footing on the greasy boards—and the stage was ready. Below the scaffold stretched a vast ocean of upturned human faces, pale, strained, eager; anxious spectators clung to roof-ridges, parapets, railings and the tops of stationary vans; while a pathetic procession emerged from the kitchens, functionaries, jailers and official witnesses, all surrounding the knot of condemned men, cadaverous, pinioned and "literally as white as marble."

[59]

Calcraft—for that was the name of the executioner —now proceeded to do his work with a ghastly nimbleness all the more surprising when one considered his advanced age. Heads were shrouded, ankles were strapped, finally a hempen noose was slung around the neck and attached to a hook that dangled from a crossbeam. "The silence was now awful. One felt one's heart literally in one's mouth, and found oneself involuntarily saying 'They could be saved yet—yet— yet.'" . . . Suddenly a muted crash that reverberated through the street announced that justice had been done; and Calcraft, fastening himself in turn on the seven victims' feet, proceeded to pull his hardest till he was satisfied that their struggles were over. An hour passed before the bodies were cut down; and, in the interval, the mob, which during the actual business of the execution had remained tense and silent, redoubled its brutality and uproar. "*Calcraft, Calcraft, he's the man*," they chanted in drunken chorus. Presently, a number of "respectable old city men" joined the crowd, trying to thread their way to offices and counting-houses. Gangs of pickpockets immediately attacked them; and, while two thugs held the indignant merchant's arms, their confederates ran neatly through his pockets. Watches, chains, scarfpins were whipped out of sight; shouts of "Murder," "Help," "Police" were uttered in vain; "the barriers were doing their duty too well, and the hundreds of constables within a few yards were perfectly powerless to get through the living rampart."

Such were the concomitants of a public hanging. In May 1868 a public execution was held outside Newgate for the last time. During September of the same year Newgate had its first private hanging; and journalists who were admitted to view the spectacle observed that there was "little to record beyond the absence of the usual execution incidents." Disraeli's reform had swept away all the scandalous and riotous aspects of the scene, substituting a more matter-of-fact horror. "There was no uproar [wrote a journalist], there were no barriers, and above all there was no wolfish crowd of thieves and prostitutes waiting to see a man die; the catcalls, the bonneting, the preaching of ministers whose every word used to be interrupted by obscenity and blasphemy; the wild jumping dances to profane choruses were all absent. There was not even a policeman; the windows opposite the jail were all untenanted, and in these days when people get compensation for all improvements it is almost wonderful that the owners or occupiers of these houses did not apply for indemnity for the loss they suffered from the criminal being hanged in private. In front of the Old Bailey, a little group of people, not a hundred in all, were standing watching the great gaunt flagstaff, at the base of which lay a mass of black—the black flag which was hoisted when the culprit fell and remained hoisted while he was hanging."

At the execution described by the author of *London in the 'Sixties*, a party of young guardsmen, on their way to see the fun, had been surrounded by the mob, robbed of all their valuables and sent home stripped to their patrician shirts. Slumming, during the 'sixties and, indeed, much later, was still a dangerous pastime; and there were large districts of London where policemen walked two and two and no prosperous pedestrian would have ventured to penetrate. We have already mentioned the perils of the Ratcliff Highway. Seven Dials, only a minute's walk from the Strand, was the recognised haunt of pickpockets and highwaymen; "the Clock House on the Dials . . . was in those days a hotbed of villainy. The King of pickpockets there held his nightly levee, and the half-dozen constables within view would no more have thought of entering it than they would the cage of a cobra." Military swells, however, sometimes rushed in where even a hardened London policeman thought it better not to tread; and "a swaggering ass named Corrigan"—the kind of young man who frequented the night-houses of the Haymarket and Piccadilly—once laid a bet that he would walk the entire length of Great Andrew Street at midnight. His friends prepared to welcome him at the farther end, and, about an hour later, he was sighted running as fast as his legs could carry him, only a rag of shirt fluttering around his waist.

No doubt it was the background of brutality that helped to give low life—as lived by Victorian swells and dandies, in this respect not so very different from their Regency and Georgian prototypes—its own especial interest and fascination. Even a visit to the races might be an adventure; and when Lord Hastings and his hangers-on drove to Epsom a professional pugilist accompanied them in case of emergencies. From Westminster Bridge to the Downs, the entire road (we are informed) "was almost one continuous panorama of life, joviality, cheer and fun." Gaping country people leaned over dusty hedgerows; "artificial cripples" begged from the ditches; and every inn was the centre of an uproarious crowd. The Downs themselves were covered with booths and side-shows—"dancing booths and *tableaux vivants* booths; booths where sparring and booths where drinking might be indulged in freely, booths where terrible melodramas were given, gambling booths and thimble-rig booths; roulette and three-card establishments, where every vice come down from the days of Noah might be indulged in without let or hindrance."

Betting continued on a magnificent scale. And, having begun with a mention of Lord Hastings, one may conclude with a reference to that "most generous of golden calves," who ended his career by losing a hundred and three thousand pounds upon a single race. In less than six years he had run through a colossal fortune. Losing, winning, lending, scattering sackfuls of sewer rats across the dance-floor at Mott's Night-House or smashing top hats at Cremorne Gardens, he explored all the variations of success and failure. In 1867 he was greeted at Epsom with vociferous applause; a year later, when his horse had lost, with insulting catcalls. "I didn't show it, did I?" he remarked afterwards, but added that "it fairly broke my heart." He retired from the Turf, a ruined and dying man. Thus expired, at the early age of twenty-six, perhaps the last dandy in the great Regency tradition.

66   The Village Maypole, *ca.* 1860

67   Scilly Island Fishermen, *ca.* 1860

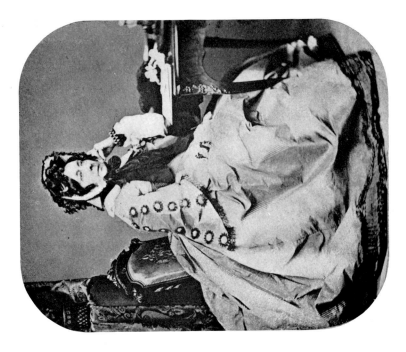

68, 69 Lord and Lady Palmerston

5

Some Victorian Characters

AN elderly friend describes how as a boy, during 'seventies or 'eighties of the last century, he remembers an old gentleman, normally self-controlled and staid, rushing into the family circle with the announcement that he had just come from a large public meeting where he had shaken hands on the platform with Mr. Gladstone! Enthusiasm transfigured his whole appearance. He seemed to walk in a glow of pride and pleasure; and the boy was both puzzled and irritated that so much virtue should proceed from a single solemn handclasp and that so much prestige should be attached to a politician. Yet the old gentleman was merely registering a capacity for enthusiasm common to his entire age. Other centuries have produced their heroes and prophets; but never has hero-worship risen to such giddy heights as at a period when great causes were matched by great men, and political eminence went hand-in-hand with moral fervour. The Victorian Celebrity is a type apart. On no other generation of great men have the obligations of greatness appeared to weigh more heavily, and seldom have those obligations been more nobly borne. Among the celebrities marshalled in this volume will be found both genuine celebrities—men and women who placed themselves deliberately in the forefront of public life—and others who achieved celebrity in spite of themselves. Here, too, are great Victorians — personages of the calibre of Gladstone and Tennyson — whose history is part and parcel of the Victorian tradition, and characters who recall the spirit of an earlier period. Thus, Lady Palmerston seems to belong, in spirit at any rate, rather to the cheerful and somewhat raffish society of her youth than to the sober world in which she passed her middle age. She had been young, as Lady Cowper, at the court of the Regent; her mother, the fascinating and cynical Lady Melbourne, had been the devoted confidante of Lord Byron, who in his letters often expresses a respectful admiration for "the Countess of Panshanger"; and some scandal had attended Lady Cowper's friendship with Lord Palmerston and the circumstances of her second marriage. In the daguerrotype here reproduced, she emerges as a Victorian dowager whose sharp face still reveals some traces of her former loveliness and an unusual share of stoical good sense: the guise under which she appeared to Mrs. Carlyle. Similarly, Brougham may strike us as a link between periods. A brilliant and indefatigable opportunist, a master of oratory and a tireless social climber, he was pilloried by Richard Doyle on the cover of *Punch* and, almost a quarter of a century earlier, terrorised and humiliated a Tory Government by his splendid, if entirely unscrupulous, defence of Queen Caroline at

72 Disraeli

71 Gladstone

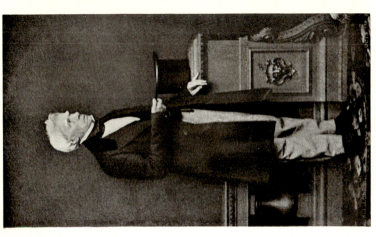

70 Brougham

74 Thackeray

73 Dickens with his Daughters

76 Tennyson

75 The Poetess, Eliza Cooke, playing Solitaire

79 Huxley

78 Newman

77 Spurgeon

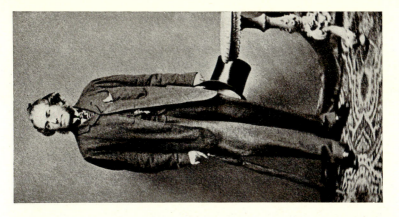

82　John Leech

81　The Traveller, G. E. Bankes

80　Lord Leighton

83 The Ambassador: Lord Elgin   84 The General: Sir Hope Grant
The Chinese Treaty of 1860

85 The Crimea, 1855: Lord Raglan and his Staff before Sebastopol

86, 87 The Crimea, 1855: Officers and Doctors behind the Lines

the Queen's Trial, when he quoted Milton to describe the King's occult influence:

> . . . The other shape,
> If shape it might be call'd that shape had none
> Distinguishable in member, joynt, or limb . . .
> The likeness of a Kingly Crown had on.

—a citation that George IV found particularly wounding, since he understood it to refer to his bulky figure.

Neither Lady Palmerston nor Brougham was essentially a Victorian; but no other period could have brought forth Tennyson, who poses for the camera, hands in pockets, head thrown back, leonine mane tumbling magnificently over a starched shirt collar, as though to embody the best traditions of poetic untidiness. Lord Leighton, by comparison, seems almost effeminate. Whiskers and beards are now regarded as truculently masculine; but Lord Leighton sports his with such a delicate and romantically self-satisfied air that we remember that not until the end of the century did men give up those arts of dressing, curling and even rouging that have now been arrogated exclusively by the opposite sex, and that a famous Victorian Chancellor of the Exchequer made a practice of going down to the House of Commons, when the time came to deliver his Budget speech, as heavily painted as an ageing beauty attending a ball.

Victorian dandies would demand a separate volume. d'Orsay's waistcoats, boots and cravats have often been celebrated; but Lord Cardigan, the hero of Balaclava and the last officer in the British Army to wear corsets, is less well known; and it seems a pity that, in a recent film travesty of the Charge of the Light Brigade, we were not shown a glimpse of its leader and his orderly-valet preparing for the field of battle. Lord Cardigan established himself throughout the campaign on his private yacht moored off the shores of the Crimea, and a picture might have been given us of his tent or cabin—the rows of cut-glass bottles containing perfumes, unguents, shampoos, the assemblage of tight-waisted uniforms; the numerous articles of toilet, tongs, brushes, tweezers and tiny whisker-combs; finally, of the heroic peer himself, setting his moustaches to rights with the help of a coroneted pocket-mirror, before he vaulted into the saddle and joined his troop, giving that famous cry: "Here goes the last of the Brudenells!"

For military distinction and a love of finery are not irreconcilable. Indeed, the character of the dandy and the character of the soldier are closely allied; and it is not going too far to suggest that the horrors of warfare—and, incidentally, the deadliness of lethal weapons—are much mitigated if opposing armies are concerned with questions of etiquette, decorum and general turn-out, and pursue warfare as a fine art rather than prosecute it as an exact science. This attitude towards war the Victorians had not entirely lost; nor were they to lose it till the Boer War banished once and for all the splendours of pipeclay and scarlet, and for the beauty and diversity of old-fashioned uniforms substituted the excruciating drabness of khaki. Some pictures of the soldier in both stages are reproduced among this collection. Fox Talbot's delightful photograph of *The Garrison at Dublin Castle in the 'Forties* shows us infantrymen wearing shakos that would not have seemed out of place on the field of Waterloo. *Soldiers of the 'Seventies*, taken outside a public-house at the bottom of Whitehall,

[68]

reveal the touch of splendour that continued to cling
to the military profession. It was South Africa that
gave modern warfare its practical grimness and
obliterated the last vestiges of folly and gallantry.

Except to journalists, the military man is no longer
a hero. He is a business-man, a technician, a
mechanic who follows a particularly dangerous and
unpleasant trade, and very soon will be indistinguish-
able from other mechanics. But in this respect the
soldier does not stand alone. Little by little all
trades, all classes, all distinctive and inherited characteristics seem to be declining, merging together, vanish-
ing away into the huge standardised monotony of
modern life, just as the entire countryside is beginning
to disappear in a gigantic suburb. Where are the
strong, hard-bitten, idiosyncratic faces often displayed
by a Victorian portraitist—the poets deliberately
poetic, the statesmen sternly noble, the soldiers self-
consciously gallant and the rustics so inveterately
rustic that we feel that they must have trimmed their
whiskers with sickles and grown their smock-frocks
and ribbed corduroys as a tree grows bark? Such
faces may explain the harshness of the Victorian universe: but they explain also the individuality, the
dignity and solidity of the Victorian achievement.

88   The Garrison at Dublin Castle in the 'Forties

Fox-Talbot

89 Soldiers of the 'Forties   *Octavius Hill*

90 Sailors of the 'Forties

Octavius Hill

91, 92 The Army in India, 1860: Fane's and Hodson's Horse

93, 94 The Crimea, 1855: Fraternisation between the English and French Armies

95 Soldiers of the 'Seventies

96 The Boer War: Lord Roberts and his Staff at Breakfast

97 The Boer War: The 1st Essex in Camp

98 Edward Sothern as Lord Dundreary

6

The Victorian Stage

No other type of human physiognomy is so distinctive, so strongly marked by the exercise of a profession, at times so interesting and so pathetic as the face of an old actor—particularly an actor who is accustomed to tragic roles. Such faces have been the battlefield of a thousand emotions; and, just as on battlefields all kinds of prosaic and homely irrelevancies exist side by side with the reminders of violence, suffering and tragic strife, so a red bulbous nose and a cadaverous unshaven jowl may accompany beetling eyebrows, lofty corrugated forehead and eyes which at the smallest provocation still roll with the concentrated malevolence of an Iago or dilate with the brooding passion of a Prince Hamlet. If the tragedians, comedians and actor managers of the Victorian age are present to us more vividly and actually than those of an earlier period, we have to thank a method of portraiture that fails to distinguish between the magnificent and the absurd, but gives us both without palliation or disguise. Both are essential to the actor's make-up; for it is the charm of his art that he should represent at once the nobility of human aspirations and the poverty of human means; that the King who carouses from an empty goblet, studded with glass jewels, in the full glare of the footlights, should retire to drink stout beneath the flickering gas of his dressing-room; that theatrical grandeurs should be off-set by theatrical miseries.

Here, perhaps, lies the secret of modern decadence. Now that acting has become as respectable a profession almost as peddling stocks and shares or governing a colony, the magnificent theatrical masks of fifty years ago have been replaced by the more or less insipid countenances of numerous ladies and gentlemen, who are equally at home on the golf course or on the boards. A true actor is the slave and victim of his calling. Grease paint sinks deep into his skin. The habit of counterfeiting emotion lends a sort of glorious insincerity—an air of high-souled and magniloquent humbug—to everything he says and does; and, though great actors are as rare as great painters or great musicians, it is one of the chief beauties of the theatrical career that every actor should, at one moment or another, give the impression that he feels that he is *great*, or that greatness is still hovering within his grasp. Modesty, respectability, social conformity are all equally out of place in the members of a caste who (here and elsewhere) have achieved their most conspicuous triumphs at a period when they were still classified as rogues and vagabonds, and have lost in importance as they have gained in position and wealth. It was during the eighteenth century that the polite, well-brushed, well-dressed actor first made his appearance; but Edmund Kean was a splendid reversion to type; and not until the latter half of the nineteenth century could the process of urbanisation and

[72]

domestication be said to have made very serious inroads. Henry Irving was the last exemplar of the grand tradition: after Irving we descend abruptly to present-day flatness.

What factors have contributed to produce this change? Obviously, several different causes have been at work; and one explanation, at least, may be found in the disappearance of the old pit which, towards the middle of the century, began to be crowded away into the back of the house by the introduction of orchestra stalls. Many an old-fashioned actor regretted its passing. The old pit was smoky, noisy, bad-mannered, but, if it was the source of cat-calls, it was also a focus of intense enthusiasm; and, "an electric communication" united players and audience. As late as 1849 "the faithful pittites" still occupied the entire floor of the Theatre Royal, Drury Lane; and an eminent Victorian critic, whose acquaintance with the Drama dated from that period, has left a vivid account of his first impressions. The benches on which the pittites sat were hard; and, between the acts, the auditorium was invaded by "women with huge and clumsy baskets filled with apples, oranges, nuts, ginger-beer, bottled stout and bills of the play, which they offered to the public in shrill, discordant voices—the very descendants of Nell Gwynne herself." Play-bills (not yet elevated to the dignity of glossy "magazine-programmes") were "long sheets of thinnish paper, vilely printed with bad ink which never seemed to dry, and that soiled the fingers and was ruination to gloves." The furnishings of the playhouse were as yet crude. The curtain was of green baize; and, in tragedies, a carpet of the same material was spread on the stage; "for it was considered

12

unorthodox and a theatrical crime to play a tragedy without a carpet of green baize."

"Give me the days when I played to the pit," Charles Mathews would lament again and again. "The stalls are profitable, but the pit was pulsating!" And, though the pit might roar and stamp its disapproval, there were no late-comers—silhouetted in haughty profile, as they waited to gain their seats at the expense of their neighbours' toes and dresses—no audibly whispered conversations, none of that languor and scarcely suppressed indifference, so characteristic of over-fed orchestra stalls. For the theatre was still largely proletarian; and, in deference to theatrical traditions and the robust proletarian tastes of a British audience, every play was served up with an accompanying side-dish. Thus, in 1849, Bulwer Lytton's *Lady of Lyons* was followed by a pantomime entitled *Harlequin's Good Queen Bess*, a burlesque of Scott's *Kenilworth*; and, after enjoying a stirring melodrama, the audience settled down to a rombustious farce— a low comedian, with a bright red wig, as Queen Elizabeth, and Lord Leicester singing a version of a popular nigger song.

Burlesques and pantomimes were shown at the licensed theatres; but the chief home of these entertainments was in the smaller theatres, or saloons. Up till 1843 only Drury Lane, Covent Garden and— during summer months—the Haymarket were authorised to represent legitimate dramas, and their suburban rivals were obliged either to diversify a play with some sort of musical accompaniment or to confine themselves to spectacular shows and knockabout comedy. It is true that these obsolete regulations— which derived their authority from a Bill introduced

[74]

101 Samuel Phelps as
Cardinal Wolsey

100 Macready

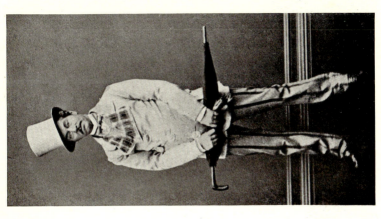

99 Charles Matthews in
L'Anglais Timide

103 Mr. and Mrs. Kendal in *The Squire*

102 Mr. and Mrs. Charles Kean, in *Macbeth*

by Sir Robert Walpole—were very often "got round"; and we read of managers who would keep a piano faintly tinkling throughout an entire play, so that a serious "drama" might qualify as a so-called "burletta." Shakespeare was often played without disguise; but farce and musical entertainment was the staple fare provided by the suburban playhouses; and some idea of its quality and diversity may be gained from a handbill of the period, announcing the reconstruction of the Grecian Saloon:

> "*Royal Eagle Coronation Pleasure Grounds and
> Grecian Saloon, City Road.*
>
> "Proprietor, Mr. J. Rouse. Unrivalled galas, with brilliant fireworks and splendid illuminations, and a series of superior amusements every Monday and Wednesday. To attempt a description of the numerous and varied sources of entertainment at this unrivalled establishment would be vain. Concerts in the open air, dancing and vaudeville in the saloon, set paintings, cosmoramas, fountains, grottoes, elegant buildings, arcades, colonnades, grounds, statuary, singing, music, to render it a fairy scene of which a due estimation can only be formed by inspection. . . . The whole under the direction of Mr. Raymond. Brilliant discharge of fireworks by the inimitable British artist, Mr. Brock. A band will play during the evening."

The Eagle Saloon—whose celebrity as a publichouse is commemorated in the famous rhyme:

> Up and down the City Road, in an' out the 'Eagle,'
> That's the way the money goes, pop goes the weasel!

was equipped with "a church organ, a grand and self-acting piano"; while seats in the auditorium were furnished with ledges to hold glasses and tankards, and the pies and bread and cheese that could be purchased in the theatre. Here seven hundred Londoners at a time might listen to a French comic opera or enjoy an English farce. The proprietor had a genuine passion for music and did his best to engage competent singers and musicians. The scenery provided was often elaborate; and every evening Mr. Rouse took his place in a box where he sat in full view of the audience, "keeping order with as much dignity as the Speaker of the House of Commons."

Even better known than the Eagle was the Olympic. Here, in 1831, Madame Vestris had launched the first of Planché's extravaganzas and burlesques; and here till 1839 she continued to produce "one-act farces, satirising solecisms in gentility and violations of elegance; two-act vaudevilles with French sentiment and Spanish intrigue; mythological and semi-poetical pieces, adapted to the display of voluptuous forms and captivating action. . . ." Five years later, in 1844, Samuel Phelps took over the management of Sadler's Wells; and, since the absurd licensing regulations had now been raised, Phelps was able to launch out on a programme far more ambitious than that of any other suburban actor-manager. His own announcement of his aims is extremely interesting: "Mrs. Warner and Mr. Phelps embark in the management and performance of Sadler's Wells Theatre in the hope of eventually rendering it what a theatre ought to be—a place for justly representing works of our great dramatic poets. This undertaking commences at a time when the stages which have been called "National" are closed or devoted to very different objects from that of presenting the real drama of England, and when the law has placed all theatres upon an equal footing of security and respectability. . . . These circumstances justify the notion, that each separate division of our immense metropolis, with its two million of inhabitants, may have its own well-conducted theatre, within a reasonable distance of its patrons."

For more than eighteen years Phelps continued to pursue the aims laid down in his preliminary notice; and during that period he not only worked his way through almost the whole Shakespearian canon but, from time to time, produced plays of a more experimental character—the dramas of modern poets (for instance, Robert Browning's *A Blot on the Scutcheon*) or plays often read but seldom acted "which if not seen at Sadler's Wells could not be seen at all." Himself, he shone in parts as diverse as Hamlet, Macbeth and Nick Bottom. Phelps was a conscientious and able performer, if hardly a comedian or tragedian of the first rank; and his photograph gives what one feels sure must have been a very faithful likeness of this enterprising and gifted man. The expression is both benevolent and a trifle saturnine; the pose genial, with a pleasant touch of professional dignity.

In Phelps's preliminary advertisement quoted above, it will be noticed that he delivers a tart reproof to the larger theatres "which are now devoted to very different objects from that of presenting the real drama of England." Naturally, some resentment against Covent Garden, Drury Lane and the Haymarket was bound to linger on; and there is no doubt that, under poor management and in hard times, these houses often resorted to representations of a spectacular and money-making kind that had very little to do with the legitimate drama. But, though chequered, their history was full of triumphs. Kean, broken in health and spirit, had retired from the stage during the year 1833. The poverty and privations of his early years, the dissipation and high living of his prosperous period had combined to bring the great tragedian to a condition of semi-insanity and complete physical collapse. On that fatal evening of March 25th, he realised that his strength had come to an end, and as the curtain rose at the beginning of the third act he warned his son Charles (who was acting with him for the first time in London) that he might need his assistance. "Mind, Charles," he said, "that you keep before me; don't get behind me in this act. I don't know that I shall be able to kneel, but if I do, be sure that you lift me up." The character that he represented was Othello. Up to his exit with Desdemona, he was able to get through the part without faltering; but when he returned, he could scarcely walk across the stage. The great "Farewell" speech he delivered with all his former eloquence; but, at its conclusion, he tottered and sank into his son's arms. "I am dying—speak to them for me," he groaned, and was carried off into the obscurity of the wings, never to re-emerge.

Thus passed perhaps the greatest—certainly the most inspiring—of nineteenth-century tragedians. By 1837—the year of Queen Victoria's accession—his fame was legendary; while the great theatrical dynasty of the Kembles had already vanished from the boards. The succeeding age has been divided into three periods. The first period, by common consent, was that of Macready. In 1837 William Charles

105 The Bancrofts in *Society*

104 Henry Neville and Lydia Foote in
The Ticket of Leave Man

107 Henry Irving in *Dearer than Life*

106 Ellen Terry: A Study by Mrs. Cameron

Macready (who had originally appeared in London more than twenty years earlier) had achieved the highest theatrical distinction. Macready's rise to eminence had neither been rapid nor easy; for both in face and in personal mannerisms he was unprepossessing; and his triumph might be described as a triumph of mind—for he was pre-eminently an intellectual actor—over the human material in which he worked. "His method [we learn from William Archer's admirable survey of Victorian theatrical progress] was eclectic, combining Kemble's long-drawn declamatory thunder with Kean's flashes of lightning. He redeemed his physical defects . . . by his great power, his irresistible tenderness, and a cultivated intelligence such as no other English actor, not even Garrick, had possessed."

When Victoria ascended the throne, Macready was just embarking on the management of Covent Garden, where he remained till 1839. One interesting feature of Macready's directorship was that no player was engaged for any particular part or line of parts; with the result that an important actor or actress might receive some comparatively unimportant role and— such was the effect of Macready's personality—accept it without complaint. The records of those two years are worth studying. Shakespeare, of course, figured largely in the bill; and Macready's Shakespearian revivals are said to have been distinguished by an elaboration of scenery and costume that was "at once gorgeous and severe." *Venice Preserved* and *The Maid's Tragedy* were also revived; while, among modern dramas, Macready scored tremendous successes with two plays by Bulwer Lytton—*The Lady of Lyons*, an immensely popular melodrama, now almost entirely forgotten, and an historical play, *Richelieu*. Yet notwithstanding his successes and the co-operation of a brilliant circle of friends, who included Bulwer Lytton, Browning, Dickens, Forster and Count d'Orsay, Macready lost money at Covent Garden and quitted the theatre—only to forget the lesson he had learned and, in 1841, assume the management of Drury Lane, where he produced *The Merchant of Venice, The Two Gentlemen of Verona, As You Like It, Much Ado About Nothing* and *King John*, "with special care," and attempted a rather unfortunate resuscitation of Byron's *Marino Faliero*. In accordance with the usual practice of the time, ambitious after-pieces—sometimes a whole opera, *La Sonnambula* and *Der Freyschütz*, sometimes a masque, *Comus* and *Acis and Galatea*, sometimes a contemporary farce—were provided to round off the entertainment. But, once again, he was obliged to admit failure and, in 1843, finally renounced the cares and glories of management amid scenes of "mad acclaim."

It was not till 1851 that Macready definitely retired from the stage he had done so much to ennoble. Like most actors, he was an unconscionable time in saying good-bye; and his farewells, which began in 1849, were protracted for the better part of two years. Then, on February 26th, he made what was, in fact as well as in the advertisements, positively his last appearance. Drury Lane was the theatre, Macbeth the part he had chosen, and he interpreted the role (to quote his own words) with "a reality, a vigour, a truth, a dignity" that he had never before achieved. His parting speech (we are told) was "brief and dignified"; the enthusiasm of the audience was unbounded; "no actor [as he himself observed] had ever received such

[80]

testimony of respect and regard in this country." There was a public dinner, with Bulwer Lytton in the chair; and thus (concludes William Archer, from whose sympathetic and lively appreciation of Macready I have already quoted) "the strenuous, thoughtful and richly endowed actor, the morose and self-torturing, but upright and warm-hearted man, withdrew into the privacy in which the remaining twenty-two years of his life were spent."

If the first period was dominated by Macready, the second belongs to Samuel Phelps and Charles Kean. Phelps's work at Sadler's Wells has been touched on in connection with suburban theatres and music halls; while Charles Kean has appeared very briefly as a participant in the last tragic episode of his father's life. But, whereas the father had genius, the son—gifted actor though he was—had talent, application and good taste. He was noted for the scrupulous accuracy of his Shakespearian revivals; and the partisans of Samuel Phelps were apt to speak of his productions in the most slighting and unfriendly terms:

"The painter, the tailor and the upholsterer [wrote one of them] are Mr. Kean's interpreters of Shakespeare. The best of their kind, no doubt, but these are servants in our school of the drama, not teachers. The palace Richard the Second lived in, the clothes he wore, and the throne he sat upon, may all be seen at the Princess's. But how about the King? . . . In life and in Shakespeare, a palace is made for a king to live in, and a throne for a king to sit upon; but at the Princess's the order of things is reversed. There a king only completes the representation of a palace, and adds by *his robes* to the grandeur of the throne. An actor at that theatre bears a strong analogy to the

wooden dummy which the tailor exhibits in proof of
his skill. The little importance which Mr. Kean
attaches to good acting needs no further proof than
the fact of his generally taking the principal character
himself. An extremely insignificant figure, a voice
without compass, depth or richness, and a delivery in
the highest degree monotonous and ineffective, are his
principal characteristics. It is not enough to say he
is not an actor; he has not a single attribute of an
actor."

Such denigration of Charles Kean's talents was
obviously unfair and ill-judged; but there is no doubt
that Kean's archaeological zeal was sometimes carried
to almost ridiculous lengths. When he produced
Shakespeare, a specially printed "archaeological fly-
leaf" was often included in the programme. Not only
did he make a careful preliminary study of the age
represented, but he even went so far as to investigate
the botany of the country in which the action of the
play was laid. Kean's attempts at Macbeth and
Othello were somewhat unsuccessful; but in the
comedies and poetic plays of Shakespeare's youth his
taste and sensitiveness found all the scope that they
required. His *Midsummer Night's Dream* was extremely
felicitous; and "nothing [declares his biographer]
could exceed the consistent harmony with which the
varied elements of the play were blended together.
The introduction to the haunt of the supernatural
beings; the first appearance of Oberon and Titania,
with their attendant trains; the noiseless footsteps of
the 'shadow-dance' on the moonlit greensward, with
the undulating reflections of every rapid and graceful
movement; the wood, peopled with its innumerable
fairy legions . . .; the melodious music composed by

110   Mario as Faust

109   Titiens as Lucrezia Borgia

108   Patti in *La Somnambula*

113 T. P. Cook in *The Pilot*

112 Charlotte Saunders in a Burlesque of *William Tell*

111 Charles Faechter as Hamlet

Mendelssohn . . . in a strain and tone of feeling in intimate sympathy with the subject; the perpetual change of scene and incident; the shifting diarama; the golden beams of the rising sun glittering on the leaves; the gradual dispersion of the mist, discovering the fairy guardians, light and brilliant as gossamer, grouped round the unconscious, sleeping mortals; the dazzling magnificence of the palace of Theseus at the close, thronged on every staircase, balustrade and corridor, with myriads of aerial beings, who join in an unseen and unheard epithalamium on the mortal inmates who have retired to rest; these, in an endless succession of skilfully blended, pictorial, mechanical and musical effects, overpowered the faculties of the spectators with the influence of an enchanting vision."

Magnificent (one can only add) but evidently not at all what Shakespeare himself had intended or foreseen! The virtuosity of Charles Kean's stagecraft made him an easy target for adverse criticism; and Kean was never a man who took kindly to criticism in any shape or form. High-minded and hardworking, but touchy, suspicious and consequential, Charles Kean was an estimable but not very lovable personage; and, reinforced by his wife, the actress Ellen Tree, who had affected a "serious and tragic air" equal to that of her husband, he enveloped his movements and utterances in all the pomposity of the old-time actor-manager, calling down fire from heaven upon the heads of those journalists and fellow-actors who were presumptuous enough to deny his genius.

In 1856, a month or two before his production of *A Midsummer Night's Dream*, Kean had revived *A Winter's Tale*; and it was in this revival that Ellen

[83]

Terry, then a little girl of eight, made her first appearance on the English stage, as Mamillius, the son of Leontes, King of Silicia, the part taken by Charles Kean himself. Well did she remember (wrote Ellen Terry in later years) the pride of that occasion. "There is something I suppose in a woman's nature which always makes her recollect how she was dressed at any especially eventful moment of her life; and I can see myself, as though it were yesterday, in my little red and white coat—very short—*very* pink silk stockings, and a row of tight sausage curls . . . clustered round my head. A small go-cart, which it was my duty to drag about the stage, was also a keen source of pride, and a great trouble to me." A theatrical photograph of the time shows the "go-cart" to have been a miniature chariot—archaeologically impeccable; while Charles Kean, who stands with one hand on the little girl's shoulder, wears cloak, robe and wreath all of the most approved archaic cut.

Charles Kean retired from management in 1859, no less a person than Mr. Gladstone presiding at his farewell banquet, and his withdrawal left a vacancy in the life of the theatre which remained unoccupied for the next ten or fifteen years. Then, gradually, the stars of Irving and Terry arose. Ellen Terry's first great success was in *The Merchant of Venice*, at the Prince of Wales under Bancroft management; Henry Irving "took London by surprise" as Mathias in *The Bells* towards the end of the year 1871. Seven years later, in 1878, Irving himself became a manager and engaged Ellen Terry (who had since added to her reputation) to act as his leading lady; and the long series of Lyceum successes began. But Irving and Terry are figures of the immediate past; their descendants are

[84]

still living; and not a few contemporary students of the drama were lucky enough to see them in person on the stage. From these observers, we learn of the incomparable fire and gusto of Irving's performance and of the "charm"—it seems impossible to find a better word—that characterised Ellen Terry's acting. Yet, in some respects, we may ask ourselves if the influence of Irving's genius was entirely beneficial. To begin with, he very often scored his most brilliant successes in entirely worthless plays, thus aggravating the breach between literature and the drama. Secondly, he popularised—if he did not initiate—the pernicious "star system" of the present century, building his productions round himself and himself alone. Members of his company grew secretly mutinous; and, eventually, during a rehearsal of *The Corsican Brothers*, the boldest member of the caste dared to put his resentment into words. "Don't you think, Governor, [he remonstrated] a few rays from the moon might fall on me? Nature, at least, is impartial!"

.　　　.　　　.　　　.　　　.

Such were the three periods—Macready's, Kean's and Phelps's, Irving's and Terry's—into which the history of the Victorian theatre has been broadly divided. Taking the age as a whole, we notice that the theatre became steadily more prosperous; that salaries rose;[1] and that, as the pit made way for the orchestra stalls, the theatrical profession gained in social prestige but lost something of its independence and early vitality. The level of theatrical taste did not improve. While discussing Macready, Kean and

---

[1] At the beginning of the century, a celebrated comic actor had considered a weekly income of seventeen pounds "*stupendous* and *magnificent*."

Phelps, we have paid particular attention to their Shakespearian revivals; for the new plays in which they appeared were usually indifferent stuff; and, when they attempted to produce the work of contemporary dramatic poets, their efforts were generally rewarded with financial failure. Macready could make nothing of Robert Browning; and the most popular dramatists of the age were the authors of melodramas, social comedies and comedies and burlesques adapted from the French. Expensive and elaborate pageantry never lost its attraction; but, here again, what at first sight we might consider evidence of typically Victorian bad taste proves to have originated at a much earlier period. From the beginning of the century, English audiences had demonstrated their liking for spectacles, processions and wild-beast shows; and in 1803 we hear that *The Caravan* achieved immediate popularity at a moment when Drury Lane was confronted with ruin, "not by reason of its character or its wit, but because a real dog, Carlos, after a good deal of coaxing, was persuaded nightly to rescue a heroine from a tank of water." Similarly, in 1836, a dramatist discovered, to his intense indignation, that in order to ensure the success of his Oriental tragedy, the manager had "engaged the Burmah bulls, elephants, ostriches, I think, and heaven knows what besides, from the Surrey Zoological Gardens."

In the theatre, then, as elsewhere, the achievement of the Victorian age was extremely unequal. The presence of fine actors was counterbalanced by the absence of good plays: the growth of taste in some directions—for example, in the presentation of Shakespeare, at length freed from the preposterous emendations imposed by Colley Cibber and others—was

116 King of the Tightrope:
Blondin

115 The Human Cannonball:
Zazel

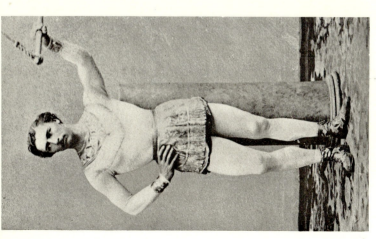

114 The original "Daring Young
Man on the Flying Trapeze":
Liotard

118　Marie Lloyd in a Cycling Number

117　Lottie Collins singing *Ta-ra-ra-boom-de-ay!*

qualified by a distinct weakening of vitality. Thus the old pit gradually disappeared; but, while the theatre became less proletarian, as "fashion"—encouraged by the Queen, herself an appreciative theatre-goer—began to congregate in the modern orchestra stalls, a new and robust form of popular amusement developed from the saloons, cider-cellars and "coal-holes" of early Victorian London. The music hall was a typical product of the Victorian genius. During the earlier decades of the nineteenth century, cheap theatres—known as "dukeys"—at which the audience paid as little as a penny a head and the proprietor might engage his leading actor at the rate of twelve shillings a week for three separate performances every evening, had offered inexpensive, noisy, exciting entertainment; and many Victorian actors who afterwards achieved distinction on a more reputable stage graduated from the squalor of the "dukey" where "dog-dramas," "melos" and fragments of historical tragedy—Gloucester in a tweed suit and Macbeth in a red coat and gold waistcoat—were dished up, behind tallow footlights, to an accompaniment of pancakes and pickled whelks. But the penny theatre, like the cider-cellar and the coal-hole, was doomed to disappear, and by the time we reach the latter half of the century and find ourselves face to face with that period of Victorian development represented so admirably by certain chapters of George Moore's *Ave, Salve, Vale,* and his immature *Confessions of a Young Man,* the music hall is our best guide to contemporary low life. It was the period of the short overcoat and the tight trouser-leg; a period, on the one hand, of intense respectability and solid family traditions—on the other, of the plump chorus girl and

[87]

of the "masher" with whom she supped at Cremorne Gardens—the period of South Kensington and St. John's Wood, at a date when South Kensington had not been broken up into a wilderness of flat-buildings and private hotels, and when St. John's Wood still embowered a multitude of charming little stucco houses in which the more prosperous merchants, noblemen and dandies maintained their theatrical sultanas.

Victorian Bohemia found its voice in the music hall. What fitter expression could be discovered (writes George Moore, in *Confessions of a Young Man*) of the "brandy-and-soda soul" of the young man of his own heyday than a music hall song, supposed to be sung by a distressed Piccadilly "stroller," with its haunting and pathetic refrain:

> Will you lend me a cab-fare, ducky?
> I am feeling so awfully queer.

Between 1850 and 1900 a huge army of different performers — equestrians, black-faced minstrels, "fashionable" singers who modelled themselves on the celebrated Champagne Charlie, wire-walkers and trapeze artists—appeared to delight and horrify the British public. There was Leotard, the original "daring young man on the flying trapeze," who combined extreme courage with "a peculiar ease and gracefulness" that caused him to make "serious inroads on feminine hearts," and who died of consumption abroad at the age of thirty. Leotard was followed by Niblo, an American gymnast of great address; while both were eclipsed by Blondin, "the hero of the Niagara," who, having made his name by crossing the Falls in 1859 and then in 1860 for the benefit of the

[88]

120 Arthur Roberts as "Gentleman Joe"

119 Frederick Robson as "Jem Bags"

121 The Finale of *The Forty Thieves*, Gaiety Theatre, 1881

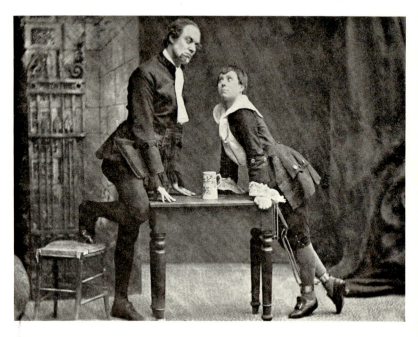

122 Nellie Farren and Fred Leslie in *Little Jack Sheppard*, 1885

future Edward VII, gave his first English performance at the Crystal Palace in June 1861, when he played the violin and beat a drum balanced high above the ground. Later, he appeared in a Crystal Palace pantomime, travestied as a monkey in *The Child of the Wreck*. It is said, however, that, for sheer dexterity, no feat of Blondin's was equal to that of Don Juan Caicedo, an exceedingly accomplished rope-walker who, "booted and spurred . . . turned a complete somersault while poised on a thin wire."

Last in the chronicle of Victorian aerialists, a place must be made for Zazel, an intrepid female performer who gained notoriety by being shot from a gun into a net at the old Aquarium Music Hall.

> It's wonderful fun
> To be shot from a gun . . .

sang the Victorian music hall ballad-monger, combining in words and tune something of that raffish gaiety and ingenuous—almost innocent—abandon so characteristic of the popular songs and ditties produced by the late Victorian age. It is difficult to re-evoke the quality that placed Dan Leno and Marie Lloyd at the head of their profession, that gave them a permanent place amid the lesser immortals of the Victorian stage. Their photographs, nevertheless, may bridge a gap. Dan Leno's face, with the huge mouth stretched in a sardonic yet good-natured smile from ear to ear, with the sharply dented chin and the wrinkled, rather simian forehead, explains the character of his Cockney humour better than any effort at description; while a portrait of Marie Lloyd, splendid in ostrich feathers and short frilly skirts, helps us to understand both the temperament of the audience and the genius of the woman by whom they were delighted. We re-live her existence off the stage—the whelks, champagne, robust vulgarity and careless open-handed generosity—and we imagine the triumphant effect of her most rousing songs—that mixture of innuendo and unblushing innocence, as different from our modern conception of popular humour as the atmosphere of a modern American cocktail-bar from the dusky-golden, gloomy yet glittering illumination that glorifies the sanctum of an old-fashioned pub.

123　Miss Marie Tempest in the Fashion of 1900

124 Patti, in the Fashion of 1863

7

Victorian Fashion

THERE was no such thing as an ugly fashion, declared Charles Baudelaire, in his magnificent essay, *Un Peintre de la Vie Moderne.* To a poet, he concludes, fashion is always interesting; since it is through fashion that we apprehend most vividly the spirit of the age— that incalculable element which provides the background of painting, music, sculpture, the element from which the artist, no matter how disinterested and unworldly, can never quite escape.

There is perhaps as much to be learned in the variations of a skirt-line—the changes of the feminine silhouette—as in many manuals that profess to record the developments of literature and the vicissitudes of contemporary thought. During the Regency, a period characterised by vitality, brutality and a certain insecurity of taste, women with their puffed shoulders, large bonnets (crowned by a huge flourish of waving ostrich feathers) and short, full skirts, suggested an assemblage of gaudy whipping-tops. During the 'thirties, on the other hand—a decade that saw the inception of the French Romantic Movement and the accession of Queen Victoria—more elegiac fashions came into vogue. The bouncing ostentation of an earlier period was replaced by an air of fly-away charm —what a fashion-writer of the time described as the "look of ideal seraphicity."

Skirts grew steadily longer and more voluminous; and from 1840 they were usually worn in conjunction with several layers of petticoat, starched muslin, corded calico, thick flannel; while a roll of plaited horsehair beneath the outer petticoat ensured the proper degree of solidity and amplitude. Though imposing, the result was far from comfortable; and, when modern ingenuity came to the rescue with the crinoline—a light framework of steel wires, substituted for the clumsy horsehair skirt—the new idea proved so popular that it earned the lucky inventor almost a million francs in less than a month!

For twenty years—till 1867, when it eventually disappeared—the crinoline maintained an undisputed ascendancy in the world of fashion. In 1860 the skirt measured ten yards round; and during the previous year it was calculated that some eleven hundred yards of material were needed for a tulle dress consisting of four skirts, trimmed with ruches. Soon the lower limbs, those provocative but unromantic appendages, which during the Regency, had revealed themselves either through the thin and clinging material of the dress or as a glimpse of plump calves clad in white stockings and high coloured boots, were entirely lost to view. The trend of later fashions was essentially Romantic. Henceforward, woman was not a two-legged viviparous animal, but an exquisite and unreal being who moved, without any apparent means of locomotion, in a perpetual sighing rustle of silken drapery. At most, a tiny foot might sometimes appear, emerging mousily from beneath the folds of a heavy skirt.

The importance given to the upper and more ethereal parts of the body was proportionately great. Rising "like a lily-stem out of a flower-tub," its comparative fragility was enhanced by tight-lacing, till the waist itself suggested a flower-stalk just where the stalk meets the corolla. It is easy to see how this fashion reflected the Romantic attitude towards helpless and unprotected womanhood. Never before had woman enveloped her charms in so much pomp, circumstance and elaboration as during the Victorian epoch; and, as the sentimentalism of the period became more pronounced, so did the crinoline accumulate new flounces, ruches, fringes—an elaboration that was shared by rich and poor, by peasant girls working in the fields (noted a German critic of 1865) by famous actresses, expensive courtesans, by respectable middle-class mothers of families and by the *grandes dames* of London, Paris and Vienna, who had observed at close quarters the magnificent crinolines of the Empress Eugénie.

Since the main article of woman's dress was stereotyped—the crinoline contracted or expanded, but did not vary its outline for some twenty-five years—originality found scope in a multitude of fresh materials, novel trimmings and agreeable minor effects. We have spoken of the poverty of Victorian taste; but it must be allowed that, in this one particular, evidence of taste, discrimination and originality is by no means lacking. The Victorian age produced many beautiful stuffs, shot, marbled, clouded, spotted, checked and brocaded, or designed in the ingenious tartan patterns that had been inspired by an affection

—common to the whole of Europe—for the novels and poems of Walter Scott.

Heavy silks and brocades were manufactured by the industrious but underpaid weavers of Lyons. Hence came "gold and silver brocades, figured with bunches of flowers in coloured silks; lampas figured with golden palms, brocatelles with embroidered flowers in gold and silver thread, and *moiré* antique of every colour" —all stuffs that owed their popularity to the Empress Eugénie, one of the first European royal personages who undertook the commercial side of her functions in a truly serious and intelligent spirit. For light summer dresses there was a large range of materials, distinguished by a variety of characteristic and charming names—crape, gauze, *barège*, muslin, grenadine, jaconet, organdie, tulle and tarlatan; while, in 1852, "crystallised" gauze appeared on the market, accompanied by "tarlatan sewn with gold and silver stars." And these diaphanous fabrics, "which were usually mounted on silks of like colour," helped to give the woman who could afford to wear them a look of being too fine, too virginal, too evanescent for the ordinary sensual uses of everyday life.

On the whole, though, our picture of Victorian elegance is summed up in the vision of a woman whose crinoline rustling and bundling behind her, seething and whispering around her feet, suggests a stately ship under full sail.

> Quand tu vas balayant l'air de ta jupe large,
> Tu fais l'effet d'un beau vaisseau qui prend le large,
> Chargé de toile, et va roulant
> Suivant un rhythme doux, paresseux, et lent . . .

wrote Baudelaire, in *Les Fleurs du Mal*. Thanks to

Fox-Talbot

125, 126 Fashions of the Late 'Thirties

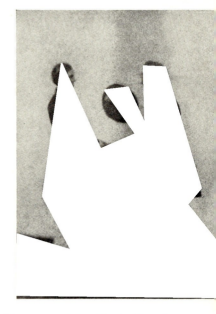

127, 128, 129   Modes and Manners of the Early 'Forties

Fox-Talbo

Romanticism, woman had assumed the majesty of an almost supernatural apparition, her bell-shaped "pagoda" sleeves, costly frilled bertha, multiplicity of mysterious and elaborate petticoats—every detail of her costume conspiring to increase the touch of awe with which she was regarded by the ingenuous, possessive male, who respects the female in proportion as he finds it difficult to approach her.

The advantages, at least from a feminine point of view, of the Romantic and idealistic attitude towards feminine beauty need scarcely be underlined. There were disadvantages too. . . . When the crinoline had reached its greatest degree of expansion, it was extremely hard—indeed, practically impossible—for more than two ladies to manœuvre their skirts in one small room. "It was necessary," remarked a lady of the Empress Eugénie's court, in later years, "to watch one's every movement carefully, to walk with a gliding step, and to supply the elegance lacking to the outline by a certain yieldingness of figure. . . . It was not easy for a woman to walk with such a mass of material to carry along with her. . . . But as to sitting, it was a pure matter of art to prevent the steel hoops from getting out of place. To step into a carriage without crushing the light tulle and lace fabrics required a long time, very quiet horses, and a husband of extraordinary patience! To travel, to lie down, to play with the children, or indeed merely to shake hands or take a walk with them—these were problems which called for great fondness and much goodwill for their solution."

Women, moreover, with the introduction of the most advanced Victorian fashions, had become highly inflammable. Though gasoliers now lighted ballroom

and drawing-room, in place of the crystal chandeliers
and silver sconces of the Georgian epoch, candles and
oil lamps were still set in dangerous proximity to
flimsy shawls, sleeves and skirts; and the chronicles of
the nineteenth century are full of stories of dreadful
deaths by fire—of how the Duchesse de Maillé was
burnt to death at a friend's fireside; how the Arch-
duchess Mathilde, discovered smoking, attempted to
hide the surreptitious cigarette in her petticoat and
went up in flames; how a French actress was inciner-
ated on the stage; and how Queen Victoria's daughter,
the Princess Royal, narrowly escaped death by the
same agency!

.   .   .   .   .

But Reason and Fashion have never been friends.
For Fashion follows a far profounder impulse; and it
is that impulse—not any considerations of convenience
or common sense—which sets women's skirts contract-
ing or expanding, raises them so that they barely cover
the knee or drops them so that the legs move beneath
the almost rigid shelter of a hemisphere of muslin,
steel and flannel. On several occasions the news
flashed across Europe that the crinoline was dead.
But it did not die. Instead, a gradual process of
transformation raised the skirt in front and elongated
it into a long and sumptuous trail of drapery that
swept the floor behind. Little by little, the over-
skirt was looped up. Slowly, it grew narrower about
the feet and knees, and more and more voluminous
about the hips; as the mid-Victorian crinoline contracted into the familiar silhouette of the late Victorian
bustle.

While the growth and decadence of the crinoline

130 Conversation Piece, *ca.* 1845

Octavius Hill

131 The Three Sisters, *ca.* 1845   *Octavius Hill*

132 Ringlets and Tartan, *ca.* 1845   *Octavius Hill*

133, 134 Fashions of the Late 'Fifties

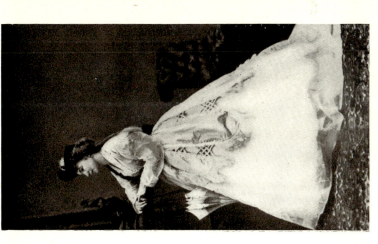

135, 136, 137 Fashions: Late 'Sixties to Early 'Seventies

138 Hairdressing Styles of the Later 'Forties

139, 140 Hairdressing Styles of the 'Seventies

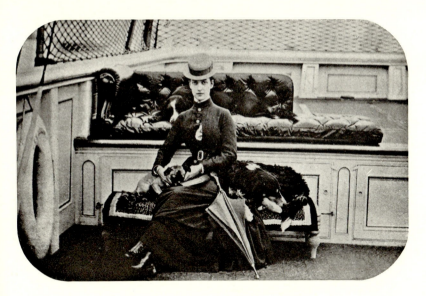

141 A Yachtswoman of the 'Eighties: H.R.H. The Princess
of Wales

142 Morning Dress in the
'Sixties

143 Evening Dress in the
'Seventies

145   Volunteer Uniform of the 'Sixties

144   Travelling Dress of the 'Sixties

147 "Collars and Cuffs": The Duke of Clarence in the 'Eighties

146 An *Elégant* of the 'Seventies

148 Ascot Fashions, 1900

corresponded to the crescendo and gradual diminu-
endo of the Victorian Romantic movement, the bustle
was the product of an age in which agnosticism,
impressionism and naturalism had already begun
to make considerable headway. Comparatively, the
bustle was almost immodest. No longer could women
float over the ground. By emphasising the hips, the
bustle imparted a provocative undulation to every
stride and, by accentuating the posterior parts of the
body, gave a steatopygous charm to the primmest
figure.

Having sighted the bustle, we enter the universe of
Charles Keane and Du Maurier, with its languid
swells, preposterous aesthetes (posed against a background of blue china and Japanese screens), popular
young curates, formidable dowagers and tennis-
playing virgins. If it had performed no other service,
the crinoline had at least prevented women from
taking part in any sport more unfeminine than croquet
or archery; but, with its disappearance, lawn tennis
and, after a time, even rowing and hockey came into
vogue, and the world rubbed its eyes at the spectacle
of heated, agitated young women stumbling in heavy
skirts across the playing-fields of England and America,
brandishing ineffectual bats and sticks.

Did these innovators really enjoy the sports in which
they could only engage at the cost of losing hair-
pins, breath, modesty? Mrs. Amelia Bloomer had
attempted to popularise the fashion that went by her
name in 1851; but her efforts were unsuccessful. And,
though the ladies of William Morris's circle had refused
to truckle to the tyranny of the crinoline and had
decorated the Red House clad in flowing loose-
waisted garments of "simple, artistic" cut, reformed

fashions had very little influence, and, till 1914, corsets, in one shape or another, were still considered absolutely indispensable. Indeed, we were many of us brought up to the belief that, if our mothers, aunts and grandmothers discarded their armoury of buckram and whalebone, they would droop and collapse like so many snow-women exposed to the full glare of the sun. It needed discipline to produce a waist of the proper circumference and round off the sculptural outlines of a perfect "bust."

Whereas "bosom" is Victorian, "bust" is the Edwardian, the former being an expansive Romantic affair, the latter more prudish but more suggestive. A Press photograph of an Ascot crowd of the 'nineties concludes the procession that begins with the first dim daguerrotypes and calotypes. The Victorian spirit has vanished; and the elegance of Victorian fashion has been supplanted by a degree of tasteless ostentation that recalls the Regency and suggests the accumulated wealth, arrogance and power of five prosperous and imperialistic decades. How sleek is the shine on the top hats! How voluminous yet how correct the frock coats! How self-confident these hats and veils and parasols! Over it all glows the late sunshine of Victorian prosperity, not yet clouded by the disasters and follies of the Boer War.

149   A Royal Shooting-party in the 'Eighties

150   A West Country Harvest Gathering, 1869

151 Queen Victoria, with the Prince Consort and the Royal Family,
opening the Crystal Palace in 1853

8

𝔙ictorian 𝔗aste

(THE GREAT EXHIBITION)

𝔄 SUBJECT as large, complex and imposing as the Victorian age—and the development of what we have come to regard as the Victorian character—may be approached from several different angles; and of these not the least effective is from the outside. The *causes* of the phenomenon were extremely various. But for the moment let us forget causes in favour of effects and, abandoning any attempt at analysis, political or sociological, confine ourselves to outward appearances, to the study of Victorianism, as it might have impressed an observer who returned to London about the middle of the century after a long stay in some inaccessible foreign land, or who rose from the dead in time for the Great Exhibition of 1851, having slumbered quietly underground since the accession of Queen Victoria.

Suppose that he paid his first visit to the huge conservatory building, designed by Joseph Paxton, that humped itself, glittering, tasteless and solid, among the elm-trees of Hyde Park. Thanks to the art of photography, then eleven years old, we can enjoy a very vivid impression of the interior of the main hall; for a daguerrotype is extant that depicts the Queen, accompanied by the Emperor Napoleon and the Empress Eugénie, seated on a platform amid palms, potted ferns, gigantic groups of sculpture carried out in dead-white Carrara marble—all dwarfed by the intricate girders of the iron roof. It is a pity that no photographer attempted to make a complete photographic record of the whole exhibition; but *The Crystal Palace, An Illustrated Cyclopaedia* (published in 1852) does its best; and its plates show us the workings of Victorian ingenuity, applied to furniture, fabrics, sculpture and miscellaneous and costly *objets d'art*, intended to decorate the prosperous Victorian home.

Never before had such a profusion of expensive merchandise been gathered together under the same roof. "The Great Exhibition . . .," wrote a Victorian journalist, on the eve of its closing, "is an achievement, the beneficial effects of which are not for our own day only, but 'for all time.' That congress of the highest practical and speculative intelligences of the various nations of the world, that vast assembling of natural products, of mechanical appliances, and of manufactured goods from all quarters of the globe, must have led to a reciprocation of individual experiences, an interchange of thought, which must add largely to the general store of knowledge, and an acknowledgment of relative commercial interests which cannot but promote the common weal of the whole human community." The social lesson to be deduced was equally comforting. "In this great mart of intelligence and wealth, the poorest of our fellows share equally, perhaps more largely, in proportion, than the richest in the land; for it is by the stimulus thus given to the energy and enterprise of the world that they must hope to improve their condition, and rise in the scale of society." *The Last Days of the Exhibition* inspired the same journalist to an even finer and more ambitious flight. The crowds that thronged the building had been vast. "In the presence of such an assemblage of human beings the highest triumphs of industry and art are forgotten, and the mind has only time to think of that great mass of humanity tendering its homage at the shrine of Labour, and vindicating the nobility of toil. . . . That nearly 110,000 people should within one day and under one roof have enjoyed the grandest spectacle that the world has ever witnessed is of itself a sufficient marvel, but that they should have done so without a single known casualty to life or property is almost incredible. So, however, it is, and we leave to revolutionary and discontented minds the study of facts which place in so clear and unquestionable a light the love of order and the genuine kindliness of spirit which pervade all classes of our population."

The results of that last week had, indeed, been "gratifying and surprising." More than five thousand pounds had been taken at the door every day, except Thursday, which was very wet, when the receipts fell to £4,344 7s. 6d.

"Nothing like it has ever been witnessed before, nor can such a spectacle be soon repeated. The excitement was not confined to the building itself, but was manifested in every part of the metropolis. The six railway termini were regularly choked up with arrivals from the country. Omnibuses were filled inside and out with a rapidity which far out-stripped the zeal of their conductors. . . . Cabs were frequently not to be had on the best-attended stands, and the thoroughfares leading to Hyde Park were swept throughout the day by a continuous and inexhaustible stream of public and private conveyances of all descriptions, including innumerable vans and carts. . . . Amid all the apparent hubbub and confusion order prevailed, and so complete were the arrangements for preventing injury to life and limb . . . that at the principal crossings policemen were stationed to watch over the safety of the timid and the aged. Till long after midday the pavements on either side along Piccadilly, and from Hyde Park Corner and up Sloane Street to Knightsbridge, were swarming with dense black columns of pedestrians, all wending their way to the Crystal Palace. Within, the vast area of the nave and transept could be compared to nothing so aptly as to a stupendous beehive; it was alive with human beings, who moved to and fro and defiled along side-aisles and clustered in courts and galleries, while the hum of their voices and the sound of their footfalls rose in one continuous swell upon the ear, impressing upon the mind of the listener mingled sentiments of awe and mystery."

The effect of this description is supplemented by an engraving of the tumultuous scene at Hyde Park Corner where a torrent of hurtling omnibuses and cabs meets the throng of aristocratic carriages attempting to leave Hyde Park .

From the opening day—when the Queen, wearing

152 The Sculptor, *ca.* 1845   *Octavius Hill*

153, 154   Fashionable Interiors of the 'Nineties at Mrs. Langtry's
London Residence

the ribbon of the Garter and leading the Prince of
Wales (in Highland costume) by the hand, and the
Prince Consort, in full uniform, flanked by the
Princess Royal, had made their way down a red
carpet between ranks of venerable beefeaters—to that
last indescribably exciting week—when the aged Duke
of Wellington (within a year of his death) was obliged
to totter hastily out of the building to escape the
enthusiasm of an over-excited crowd—the Exhibition
had been a vast and spectacular triumph. A new
epoch seemed to have opened in the world's history.
After the troubled years with which Victoria's reign
had begun—and the threats of revolution that per-
sisted throughout the 'thirties and 'forties, till the
Chartist movement reached an inglorious climax in
the year of revolutions, 1848—Englishmen looked
ahead to a golden age of wealth and concord, as the
blessings of industrial civilisation gradually penetrated to the very lowest and most depressed stratum
of the community. Palmerston himself, a hard-
headed veteran of four reigns, declared that the
Exhibition was the greatest and most significant
event he had lived to witness. The scheme, as
originally propounded, had aroused fierce opposition;
but all criticism was silenced by the brilliant result;
and the Queen's emotion as she contemplated her
husband's handiwork had its counterpart in a sudden
burst of national pride. There was one rebel, however, at the Crystal Palace. Many years were to go
by before William Morris could claim that he had
made much progress towards the re-education of
Victorian aesthetic taste; and meanwhile, as a very
young man, the son of a well-to-do bill-broker, he
stared aghast at the appalling ugliness of the objects

exhibited, the heaviness, tastelessness and rococo banality of the entire display. But Morris was still a rebellious exception; and it is possible that our judgment will be more accurate if we return to the point of view of an imaginary observer who re-visited London, after a long absence, in 1851.

Some feelings of admiration he could scarcely escape. Within two decades, civilised man had invented for himself more new playthings than had fallen into his lap during the previous five hundred years. What a wealth of opportunity, what an extraordinary enlargement of human consciousness, this new machinery of life appeared to offer! It was only when he came to examine the aesthetic products of the period that an observer would have realised that the general rate of progress had been extremely uneven—that humanity, striding forward in some directions, had fallen back, or at least remained stationary, in many others. Romanticism still moulded public taste; and our observer, wandering at will through the galleries, transepts and cloisters of the Crystal Palace, observing the intricacy, splendour and picturesqueness of the wares exhibited, might have assumed that the country he had deserted twenty years before was now inhabited by a race of semi-Oriental nabobs—desperate but tasteless Romantics who expressed the eccentricity of their interests by the wildly conceived, oddly executed furniture among which they passed their lives—that every merchant's villa was a miniature Fonthill.

Romanticism has always inclined to exaggeration; and he would have been surprised by the preponderance of very large and very small objects. Huge groups of sculpture towered overhead in every room.

A colossal statue of Queen Victoria in zinc was balanced by a gigantic Godfrey de Bouillon. Kiss's *Amazon Attacked by a Tiger* was designed on an equally heroic scale, and "received more tributes of unqualified praise than perhaps any other single object in the Crystal Palace. It is certainly a very masterly production, and in a style which is almost new to sculptors of our day; though, at the same time, from the nature of the subject, it is not entitled to rank with works in the highest class of sculpture. It is more animal than spiritual; the conception more startling then poetic. For the Amazon, it is a figure of tremendous energy. The manner in which she is represented, as having thrown herself back out of her ordinary seat, in order to get beyond the reach of the tiger . . . whilst she takes deliberate aim for a single and critical blow at the head of the savage monster, is admirably conceived and carried out; the face with its mixed expression of terror and determination, is of itself a study sufficient for an entire work of sculpture. The horse and tiger are both masterpieces in their own way, but unfortunately more than divide the interest with the human subject."

So much for works of art that impressed by their bulk. Yet it is a curious fact that, as we look through the illustrations of the *Cyclopaedia*, before we have had time to refer to the letterpress, we are often at a loss to distinguish between the minute and the colossal; for the scheme, execution and general feeling of a gigantic group of sculpture in marble or bronze and some elaborate silver centre-piece, intended to grace a rich man's dinner-table or sideboard, are strangely alike. No real sense of proportion, no sympathy for the material of the work—whether it be zinc, bronze, marble or filigree silver—guided the artist: his inspiration was literary and romantic; he might glory in the number of cubic feet occupied by nymph, shepherdess or warrior-angel, but he did not pause to inquire if the dimensions of a work of art might not have some important, though hidden, connection with the reality of the design.

The Victorian artist triumphed in the defeat of his material and was proud to show that no mere practical considerations had hampered the high-minded romantic *élan* with which he had addressed himself to the undertaking. The decorative licence his public allowed him was wide; for, as means of communication grew more and more efficient—puffing locomotives and churning paddle-steamers bringing home every day the arts and manufactures of the farthest corners of the globe—new *motifs* were constantly entering the artist's repertory, till there were very few objects of use or virtu that did not display traces of several quite different and often entirely irreconcilable aesthetic styles. Since the beginning of the eighteenth century, the East had made lavish contributions to the formation of Western taste; but its products had usually been assimilated to the European mode and had been absorbed by a living contemporary tradition. Baroque art at its most extravagant seems almost restrained when its manifestations are set alongside some of the more elaborate masterpieces of an ambitious Victorian manufacturer. For, whereas the baroque artist commonly employed *motifs* indigenous to Europe and characteristic of the period in which he worked, Victorian taste expressed itself in the collection and wilful conglomeration of *motifs* borrowed from every period and every country

In the French Section

The Ellenborough Testimonial Silver Service, by Hunt and Roskell

A Sideboard, by Jackson and Graham

A Cast-Iron Balustrade, by Baily and Sons

under the sun, in the wildest and most fantastic confusion of epochs.

A fine and representative example of Victorian aesthetic symbolism is provided by the Ellenborough Plate, a silver dinner-service, made by Hunt and Roskell, to be "presented to the Earl of Ellenborough, by his lordship's friends in India." Though it consists of only seven pieces in all, this service finds room for no less than twenty-seven carefully wrought figures, human and animal, seven camels, three elephants, a rhinoceros, a lion, five sepoys, a Chinese captive, an Afghan, two river gods, two nymphs, and a pair of classical figures which represent Asia crowning Britannia; while the centre-piece, of vaguely Indian design, is embellished with *bassi relievi* which depict the ratification of the Treaty of Nankin, and contains views of Calcutta, Kabul and Canton. A wealth of exotic vegetation sprouts from every crevice; and the twin candlesticks have twisted rustic stems, subdivided into numerous and intricate branches.

Even more impressive were the workings of Victorian fancy when unrestricted by the need for symbolic expression. Much in evidence among the manufacturers who exhibited at the Crystal Palace was the Coalbrookdale Company, whose greatest achievement (housed in the vast Western Nave) was an Ornamental Ironwork Dome, some thirty feet high, sheltering a life-size statue, Bell's *Eagle Slayer*, the eagle slayer's quarry, a dying bird of prey transfixed by an arrow, being attached to the inner surface of the cupola. The entire fabric was constructed of elaborately interwoven cast-iron tracery, running up into a tangled roof of iron foliage and supported on six massive rustic boles. Opinions were divided as to its merits; and the *Cyclopaedia*, for once taking a critical and independent tone, observed that, although it did credit to the founders and was, in some ways, "remarkably pretty," there were "many and grave objections to the design, which is childish and purposeless. Though called a dome, it is merely a rustic garden house. . . . The eagle transfixed by an arrow at the top inside must be considered an absolutely inexcusable piece of bad taste."

Looking along the perspective of the Western Nave towards the Coalbrookdale Dome, the eye of a contemporary observer would have paused first at a white marble fountain—part Gothic, part classical in taste, with classical tritons, Gothic-Romantic figures and semi-Gothic vegetable incrustation: next at Mrs. Rosse's Stone Cross, a neo-Celtic affair carved in solid granite: lastly, at Dent's Turret Clock. Gothic influences were widespread throughout the whole exhibition; and the Gothic Court contained some of the choicest specimens of that revived taste for medieval architecture which had originated in the dilettante experiments of Horace Walpole and William Beckford. Here the Victorian tendency to improve on, rather than imitate, Gothic models is particularly evident; and an interesting comparison might be drawn between an architectural Gothic bookcase (the property of Queen Victoria) and the almost equally ponderous but slightly less extravagant Gothicism practised half a century earlier by Pugin and Wyatt.

It was Romantic literature that had fostered the Gothic revival; and to the same source—particularly to the novels of Sir Walter Scott—may be traced the many "Elizabethan" objects, wall-brackets,

[108]

sideboards, mantelpieces and tables, in which the Victorian woodworker displayed his skill. Among the glories of the Exhibition—"one of the chief lions on the British side"—was the Kenilworth Buffet, made from the wood of a colossal oak-tree felled near Kenilworth Castle. The magnificence of this "very carefully studied and ambitious work" is best conveyed by some extracts from a detailed contemporary description. "The subject of the design [wrote the makers] is the Kenilworth Pageant of 1575, in honour of Queen Elizabeth's visit to the Earl of Leicester, described by Laneham and Gascoigne . . . and vividly reproduced by Scott. The design of the centre panel, carved out of one solid block of oak, represents Queen Elizabeth entering Kenilworth Castle, in all the pomp usually displayed on these occasions . . . Leicester is bareheaded and on foot, leading the horse upon which his august mistress is seated, magnificently arrayed. . . . Two pages and a long train of attendants follow the Queen and her host, composed of ladies, statesmen, knights, and warriors—some on foot, others on horseback. In the distance are soldiers and a mixed multitude of people. A portion of the Castle is seen in the background. . . . At the opposite end of the panel, the Earl of Essex, Leicester's rival in the favour of Queen Elizabeth, is conspicuously seen, mounted on a charger. On the table part underneath the centre panel is displayed the Tudor rose. . . . On the spandrils, supported by water flowers and rockwork pendentives, are marine subjects taken from the 'Pageant' . . ." Other panels represented scenes from Scott's novel, Elizabeth meeting Amy Robsart in the grotto and the interview between Elizabeth and Leicester after her discovery of his marriage. Sidney, Raleigh, Shakespeare, Drake, appear as statuettes. "The ragged staff mouldings . . . are imitations of the best examples in the Beauchamp Chapel, Warwick"; four effigies of the Earl of Warwick's crest—the bear and ragged staff—uphold the projecting shelves; while coroneted monograms, between "specimens of Elizabethan ornaments, designed by the proprietors," add a final touch of lofty elaboration.

Gothic, Classical, Elizabethan, Moorish, Indian, Far-Eastern influences — separately, or in curious hybrid forms produced by the fusion of two or more styles of decoration—all contributed to the splendour of the Victorian background. The Renaissance reappeared, much travestied, in the detail of silverware, inlaid cabinets and tables, pottery plaques, state bedsteads, jugs and sculptured vases; the Orient made itself felt in the design of printed and embroidered fabrics; and German Classicism laid a heavy hand on the art of sculpture. Some account of the larger statues exhibited has already been given; but there were others in which sentiment made up for size; and, among these, feminine subjects were most conspicuous. Charming womanly figures claimed attention in every room. Kirk's pensive *Ariadne* was voted "a very pleasing example of the Romantic style"; John Thomas's *Rosamunda*, "without doubt one of his best works, the attitude being dignified and graceful," the costume "somewhat medieval in character, the same feeling pervading the monumental details." Nor did the Victorian sculptor shrink from nudity. *Una and the Lion, Susannah, A Veiled Slave* and *Andromeda* are equally modest and bare, suggestive and innocent. Only *Dorothea,* with rolled-up breeches on

Ormolu Clock, by Howell and James

Wine Table in Irish Bog Oak, by Jones of Dublin

" Michael overthrowing the Dragon," by Le Seigneur

girlish thighs, seems to over-step the delicate boundary line between art and voluptuousness.

But, whatever the treatment, it was the subject that came first; and an illuminating example of Victorian art-criticism, as applied to works of sculpture, is supplied by the following remarks on "Mr. Lough's equestrian plaster group, entitled *The Mourners*"—a widow and a war horse bending over the corpse of a medieval knight. The story suggested was generally considered very affecting; and "if the heart . . . [observes a critic] were the only guide to be consulted in the consideration of works of design, undoubtedly Mr. Lough might be said to have achieved a very great success. In point of sentiment, however, even of everyday sentiment, there does appear to us a little extravagance and inconsistency in placing a horse and a Christian widow in a partnership of sorrow. For even supposing the horse had a right to indulge his feelings on the occasion of the loss of a good master, as well as the bereaved wife, he might have been kept a little in the background; at least, the woman should not have been called upon to bestow any of her attentions upon the dumb animal, when she should have been exclusively engrossed with the appalling sight of a husband untimely slain. These are errors of poetic judgment which throw sentiment into ridicule, and reduce art to the level of an Astley's melodrama."

We have discussed at some length the various influences that went to form the canons of conventional Victorian taste; but it is interesting to notice that there were certain designers who had arrived at a slightly more individual style and who came near to anticipating *l'Art Nouveau*. An extraordinary product of this style is *The Dreamer's Chair in Papier Mâché*, exhibited by Messrs. Jennens and Bettridge of London and Birmingham who, beginning with papier mâché tea trays, had adapted that light and convenient material to the manufacture of tables, chests, work-boxes and even piano-cases. "Ornamented with figures, flowers, etc., allegorically arranged," the *Dreamer's Chair* suggests 1900 rather than 1850; for the sleeping figures which recline in soporific attitudes along the head-rest and sides are curiously reminiscent of those late Pre-Raphaelite genii that we admire in early numbers of the *Studio*; and the whole design has the kind of debased, yet entirely unpleasing, fluidity that characterised the pre-War Viennese school.

But it is time to turn from the Exhibition to its visitors—to the immense concourse, bonneted and top-hatted, clad in sober broadcloth or draped in the swelling splendour of crinolines, mantles and Indian shawls—with here and there the turban or the fez of some wondering Eastern dignitary—that poured day after day through the Crystal Palace. Ardent loyalists, they would have halted before the barrier that separated the public from the Queen's With-drawing Room at the North Entrance—a "little bijou of a boudoir," lined with blue and white silk, hung with costly tapestry and gay underfoot with a rich Brussels carpet—thence moving on to admire the Crystal Fountain, which stood in the centre of the Palace at the intersection of the Nave and the Transept. A kind of gigantic inverted chandelier, twenty-seven feet high, it glittered and sparkled in the sunlight of the roof, the water, which gushed from a taper central shaft, issuing in a "broad well-spread jet" and "forming in its descent a lily-like flower before separating into spray." Beneath the Coalbrookdale Ornamental Dome a pianist, surrounded by crowds of "aristocratic and attentive listeners," might be tinkling out Mendelssohn's *Spring Song*. In another quarter of the building the voices of a massed choir would be rising in a blast of harmonious exultation towards the girders of the roof, or a huge organ trolling forth its sonorous music.

It is not surprising that the spectator's emotions were kept at bubbling-point. Prince Albert had expressed a fervent hope that "the first impression which the view of this vast collection would produce . . . would be one of deep thankfulness to the Almighty for the blessings he has bestowed upon us already here below"; and thankfulness was mixed with romantic pleasure. "Unquestionably neither Eastern fairy tale nor Arabian Nights wonder could surpass, or even emulate, the gorgeous reality . . ." Several elms had been incorporated in the building; and their living foliage, imprisoned beneath the crystalline concavity of the glass and iron vault, helped to increase the effect of poetic strangeness. During the six months that it remained open, six million visitors made their way through the Crystal Palace, admiring every kind of object from the Koh-i-noor diamond (recently presented to the Queen by the East India Company) to such minor Victorian fantasies as "faery bells", thistle inkstands, writing-tables crowned with antlers, comic groups of stuffed cats and frogs, and a Comic Electric Telegraph which, says the *Cyclopaedia*, "would no doubt prove an amusing and instructive addition to the ornaments of the drawing-room, since it might be used to illustrate the principle of magnetic induction."

17 [113]

What blessings had modern science already bestowed! But these blessings, declared the Prince Consort in his introductory address, could "only be realised in proportion to the help which we are prepared to render to each other; therefore only by peace, love and ready assistance not only between individuals, but between the nations of the world." Well, the nations of the world had done their part. Every land had sent its contingent of visitors; and this foreign influx—though critics of the Exhibition had suggested that they "might become assassins by night or take military possession of London by day"— had behaved with an almost British rectitude, merely swelling the general chorus of pleasure and praise. Sad that, within three years, England, Russia and France should have found themselves committed to a bloody, costly and quite unnecessary war—that the Prince Consort should have died, his visions unrealised. Never again would Victorian prospects seem so fresh and hopeful as in that brilliant summer of 1851.

Index

(The numerals in italics denote the *figure numbers* of illustrations)

[116]